Read and Respond Journal

GRADE 2

Printed in the U.S.A.

ISBN 978-0-358-25226-9

10 2023

4500879843   r6.23

Contents

Rosa's Garden

by Carol Alexander

I am Sofia. This is Miss Rosa.
She has a garden. It is big!
Miss Rosa grows flowers.
She grows carrots and peas.
I don't eat peas. Not one pea.
No way!

READ & RESPOND

Setting

Have you ever been in a garden? What was it like?

Yes, I have been in a garden.
A garden is colorful. I
saw plants, flowers, fruits and
vegetables.

This summer, Miss Rosa fell. She
hurt her knee. Now she can't walk. She
just sits in a chair. She watches the birds.
Two shovels lie in the grass. Miss
Rosa looks sad. What would help
her feel better?

READ & RESPOND ▶   Ask and Answer Questions

Do you understand what happened to Miss Rosa?
Is there anything in the text that can help you understand?

Miss rosa fell and hurt
herknee. She sits in a chair.

I go home to think. "Mom, I need paper. I want to draw a picture."

Mom smiles. "Here is some plain white paper." She gives me a few pieces. "I can't wait to see what you draw."

READ & RESPOND   Setting

What is the setting of the story now?
Has it changed since the beginning of the story?

The setting is in sofia's house.

I find my crayons. What will I draw?
I close my eyes. The scent of flowers
blows in through the window. Now I
know just what to draw.

READ & RESPOND

Ask and Answer Questions

What do you think Sofia will draw?
What clues in the text can give you your answer?

Sofia will draw a garden.
she smells the flowers.

5

I draw and draw. Here are the sweet peas. They are blooming in May. There are the tomatoes. They are red and round.

I keep drawing. Mom says, "Your hand will fall off, Sofia!"

READ & RESPOND   Setting

Do you think the garden setting is important to the story? Explain.

The setting is important because the story is all about the garden.

At last, I am done. I find Miss Rosa.
I hand her my picture.

"This is for you," I say.

She looks at it. She smiles and hugs me.

"Do you really like it?" I ask.

READ & RESPOND

Ask and Answer Questions

How do you know Miss Rosa likes the drawing?
Use clues in the text to find your answer.

Miss rosa smiles and hugs her.

7

"Oh, yes!" Miss Rosa says. "This is the best garden. It makes me happy. Thank you, Sofia."

"Spring will come again. We can work in the garden together," I say. "We will plant lots of peas!"

Setting

What time of year do you think this story takes place? What clues on this page help you to know?

This story can take place in summer.

Reread and Respond

Way To Go

1 **Why does Miss Rosa feel sad?**

Miss rosa is sad because she fell on her knee and now she has to sit in a chair.

Hint
For a clue, see page 3.

2 **Why does Sofia draw a picture?**

Sofia draws a picture of a garden because sofia is making miss rosa happy.

Hint
For a clue, see page 3.

3 **Why does Miss Rosa like the picture?**

Miss rosa likes the picture because she can remeber her garden.

Hint
For a clue, see page 8.

9

The Nicest Party

by Maria Sanchez

I am so happy.
Uncle Takada and Aunt Onida
are coming to visit. Their daughter,
Tala, is coming, too.

I have not met Tala. I've seen
pictures. I like looking at
family pictures.

READ & RESPOND   Author's Purpose

Look at the title. Does it give you any clues about why the author may have written the story?

The author wrote this story to tell about a party.

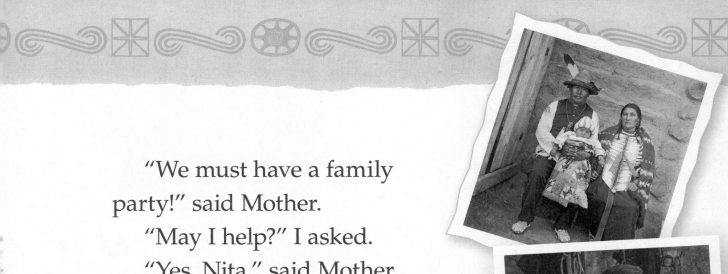

"We must have a family party!" said Mother.

"May I help?" I asked.

"Yes, Nita," said Mother. "We must shop for party things."

Photographs

READ & RESPOND   **Monitor and Clarify**

Think about a time you had a party. What kinds of things do you think Nita and her mother will buy?

I think nita and her mom will buy decorations, cake and goodie bags.

11

We went to the party store.
We got things for the table.
I remembered to get balloons.
We got a crown for Tala.
"I can't wait for the party!"
I said.

READ & RESPOND   **Monitor and Clarify**

What clues in the text can help you know how Nita feels about the party?

she feels happy to see
her tala and her uncle and
laslo her aunt

12

"We have more shopping to do," said Mother.

We went to the toy store. I saw a stuffed bear. We got it for my cousin Tala.

READ & RESPOND

Author's Purpose

Is the author trying to keep your attention so that you will be entertained? How do you know?

The author is trying to entertained. I know this because there is a setting and characters.

13

We went to the market next. We got fruit. We got vegetables. We got other good things to eat.

We put the food in our cart. Soon we had all we needed.

READ & RESPOND

Monitor and Clarify

Why do Mother and Nita go to the market?
What clues in the text help you know?

_____

_____

Then we went home.
Mother cooked. I helped.
"It smells so good!" I said.
    We put out the party
things. "Now we are ready!"
said Mother.

READ & RESPOND

Main Ideas and Details

What did Mother and Nita do to get ready for the party?

_____

_____

_____

It was party time! Everyone in our family came. We ate. We laughed. My aunt played music. Tala wore her crown.

"This is a special party!" said Uncle Takada. "Thank you!"

Author's Purpose

What was the author's purpose for writing this story?
What clues in the text help you to know?

_____

_____

Reread and Respond

1 **How do you know that Nita is excited to meet Tala?**

_____

_____

_____

Hint

For clues, see pages 12 and 13.

2 **How are the party store and the market different?**

_____

_____

_____

Hint

For clues, see pages 12 and 14.

3 **Who plays music at the party?**

_____

_____

_____

Hint

For a clue, see page 16.

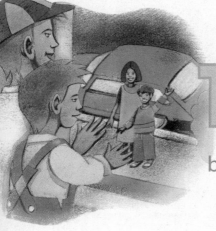

The Play Date

by Margaret Maugenest

Eric and Dylan are brothers. Raul comes to play with them.

"Let's make a spaceship," says Dylan.

"Let's play baseball," says Eric.

There is a problem. Who will get his way?

READ & RESPOND   Characters

How are Eric and Dylan related? Who is Raul?

_____

_____

_____

"I have an idea," says Raul. "Let's build a spaceship first. Then we can play ball."

Eric gets furious. "No," he says. "Making a spaceship is a baby game." Eric goes to his room. He slams the door.

READ & RESPOND ▶

Characters

How can you tell that Eric is mad?

_____

_____

_____

Raul frowns. "Let's make the spaceship. Eric will calm down. He can come later," Raul says.

Dylan and Raul go to Dylan's room. Eric hears them laugh. He puts his ear to the wall.

READ & RESPOND   Characters

How do you know that Dylan and Raul are having a good time?

_____

_____

_____

Eric hears talking.

"This is fun," says Raul.

"I wish Eric were here," says Dylan.

Eric wants to play. It is impossible for him to stay mad. He goes to Dylan's room. He peeks inside.

Characters

How is Eric feeling at this part of the story? How do you know?

_____

_____

_____

Eric sees the spaceship. Dylan and Raul
are in it.

"Blast off!" says Dylan.

"Is there room for me?" says Eric.

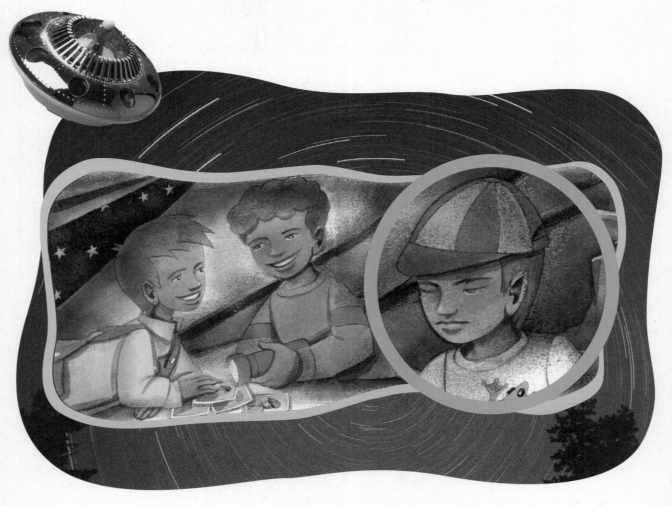

Characters

What do you think Eric wants to do?

_____

_____

_____

Dylan and Raul smile.

"Yes! Get in," says Raul. "We're off to the moon."

Eric sits in the tent. "I'm sorry I got mad," he says.

READ & RESPOND

Characters

Do you think Eric feels bad about how he acted? How do you know?

_____

_____

_____

"We didn't believe you would stay mad," says Raul.

"We'll play ball soon. We just have to get back from the moon!" says Dylan.

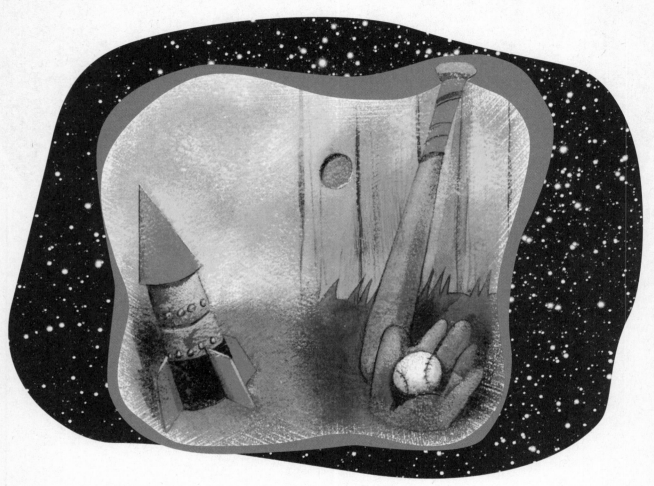

Characters

Describe one of the characters. Use the story to help you.

_____

_____

_____

Reread and Respond

1 **Why is Eric mad?**

_____

_____

_____

Hint
For clues, see pages 18 and 19

2 **Eric puts his ear to the wall. Why?**

_____

_____

_____

Hint
For clues, see pages 20 and 21.

3 **Is Raul good at getting along? How do you know?**

_____

_____

_____

Hint
See pages 19, 20, 23, and 24

Best Friends

by Margaret Maugenest

Mai and Jenny were best friends. They lived next door to each other.

A tree stood between their homes. It had a straight trunk. The top of the tree looked like curly green hair.

READ & RESPOND   Make Inferences

What makes the top of the tree look like curly green hair?

_____

_____

_____

Jenny and Mai wrote notes to each other. They put the notes in a tree. It was their secret hiding place.

It was Jenny's birthday. Mai got Jenny a present. She wrote Jenny a note.

READ & RESPOND

Main Ideas and Details

Why did Mai get Jenny a present?

_____

_____

_____

The note said to come to Mai's house. Mai put a red bow around the note. She put it in the tree. Then she waited.

Jenny did not come. Mai checked the tree. Her note was gone.

READ & RESPOND

Make Inferences

Why did Mai want Jenny to come over to her house?

_____

_____

_____

Mai looked at Jenny's house. She saw kids. They lined up in a row. They had presents. They went into Jenny's house.

Jenny was having a birthday party! Why didn't she invite Mai?

READ & RESPOND

Main Ideas and Details

What is happening at Jenny's house?

_____

_____

_____

Mai sat on her swing. She felt mad.

Jenny came. "Why aren't you at my party?" she said.

Mai got off the swing. She stood tall. "You didn't invite me!" she said.

Main Ideas and Details

Why is Mai mad?

_____

_____

_____

"I DID invite you. I put a note in the tree," said Jenny.

The girls heard a noise. They looked up. They saw a bird in a nest. The nest had paper. It had a red bow.

READ & RESPOND

Make Inferences

Where is the bird's nest? How do you know?

_____

_____

_____

"That bird took our notes. It took the ribbon. It used them for its nest!" said Mai.

Jenny and Mai still write notes to each other. Now they put their notes in a box. They are still best friends.

READ & RESPOND

Make Inferences

Why do Mai and Jenny put their notes in a box now?

_____

_____

_____

Reread and Respond

1 **Where do Jenny and Mai hide notes to each other?**

_____

_____

_____

Hint

For a hint, see page 27.

2 **Jenny is having a party. How does Mai feel?**

_____

_____

_____

Hint

For a hint, see page 30.

3 **The girls see the nest. After that, where do they put notes?**

_____

_____

_____

Hint

For a hint, see page 32.

Who Made These?

by John Berry

Snow fell. Now the tree branches are white.
Molly and her brother take a walk.
"How will we know where to go?"
asks Jeff. "Snow has covered the path."
"Don't worry," says Molly. "I can find the
way. I know these woods."

READ & RESPOND

Connect Text and Visuals

Who made the tracks in the snow on this page? How do you know?

_____

_____

_____

They walk across their yard. Jeff stops.
He points to some tracks.

"Who made these?" he asks.

"Here is a hint. It is an
animal that hops," Molly says.
"It has a round tail."

READ & RESPOND   Connect Text and Visuals

How does the illustration help you understand what Jeff is asking?

_____

_____

_____

"A rabbit?" Jeff asks.

"Right," Molly says. "It was a cottontail rabbit."

They walk into the woods. They go around trees. They go over hills. They go left and right. The path is winding.

rabbit

READ & RESPOND   Connect Text and Visuals

Look at the illustration of Molly and Jeff. Would you know what they looked like without the picture? Explain.

_____

_____

They come to a pond. Jeff finds more tracks.

"Who made these?" he asks.

"An animal with a black mask," Molly says. "It has a striped tail."

READ & RESPOND

Connect Text and Visuals

How does the illustration help you see how the footprints are different? Would you know that by just reading the text?

_____

_____

"A raccoon?" Jeff asks.

"Right again!" Molly says.

"I saw a raccoon last fall," Jeff says. "It was up in our apple tree. I guess it liked apples."

Molly and Jeff move on.

READ & RESPOND

Connect Text and Visuals

Does the illustration help you understand what Molly meant by "an animal with a black mask"? How does it help you?

_____

_____

They cross a field. Molly points to
more tracks.

"These are the deepest tracks," Jeff says.
"They go far down into the snow.
Who made them?"

"A big animal," Molly says.
"It has antlers."

READ & RESPOND Connect Text and Visuals

**Look at the illustration. How does it help you understand how these
tracks are the deepest?**

_____

_____

"A deer?" Jeff asks.

"Right again," Molly says. "These are the tracks of a big deer."

"How do you know so much?" Jeff asks.

"I'm older," Molly says. "Soon you'll be a great tracker, too."

deer

READ & RESPOND

Connect Text and Visuals

Think about the illustrations in the story. Did the illustrations help you understand the story better? Explain.

_____

_____

Reread and Respond

1 How many toes does a raccoon have on each foot?

_____

_____

_____

Hint

For clues, see pages 37 and 38.

2 How are rabbit tracks and deer tracks different?

_____

_____

_____

Hint

For clues, see pages 35 and 39.

3 What does Jeff learn on the walk?

_____

_____

_____

Hint

For clues, see pages 35 through 40.

Pat Mora

by Jean Casella

Pat Mora grew up in Texas.
She spoke two languages.
Pat spoke English. She spoke
Spanish, too.

READ & RESPOND   Central Idea

Look at the title. Whom or what do you think this text will be about?

_____

_____

_____

Pat's grandparents grew up in
Mexico. Pat spoke Spanish with them.
Pat's aunt grew up in Mexico, too.
She told stories about growing up there.
She told some stories
in English. She told
some in Spanish.
Pat loved her
aunt's stories.

READ & RESPOND

Central Idea

Why did Pat's aunt speak Spanish?

_____

_____

_____

Pat loved to read. She read about places far away. She liked to pretend she was there.

There were always books in Pat's house. Her mother would drive her to the library, too.

READ & RESPOND

Central Idea

What is the most important detail on this page? Why do you think so?

At school, all the lessons were in English. So Pat spoke English at school. She also spoke it at home.

When Pat grew up, she became a teacher. She taught kids to read and write.

READ & RESPOND

Central Idea

Name the things Pat taught her students.

_____

_____

_____

Pat had a lot of ideas. She wanted to write books. She wanted to express her ideas in words.

Pat wanted to write about growing up in Texas. She wanted to write about speaking two languages.

READ & RESPOND

Central Idea

List two facts about Pat on this page. Why are those facts important?

_____

_____

_____

Pat started to write books. Her books won a prize. Then she wrote more books.

Pat wrote about families like hers. She told stories, just like her aunt did.

READ & RESPOND   Central Idea

What does the author want you to know about Pat on this page?

_____

_____

_____

Some of Pat's books are in English. Some of her books are in Spanish. Some of her books have English words and Spanish words. They use two languages—just like Pat!

READ & RESPOND

Central Idea

What is the central idea of the text? How do you know?

_____

_____

_____

48

Reread and Respond

1 **Where did Pat's family live?**

_____

_____

_____

Hint

For a clue, see page 42.

2 **Why did Pat want to write books?**

_____

_____

_____

Hint

For clues, see page 46.

3 **How was Pat like her aunt?**

_____

_____

_____

Hint

For a clue, see page 47.

Flood on River Road

by Shirley Granahan

It rained all day. It rained all night. It rained heavily for days.

"I am sick of rain," said Jody.

"Me, too," I said. "At least we're warm and dry."

READD & RESPOND ▶   Point of View

Is Jody telling the story? How do you know?

_____

_____

_____

We looked down the hill. Water covered River Road. It spilled into Mr. Lee's house.

"This is a flood!" Mom said seriously. "We must help Mr. Lee!"

READ & RESPOND

Monitor and Clarify

Do you know what a flood is? How can the illustration help you to know?

_____

_____

Mr. Lee stayed at our house. He kept planning to go home. He had to wait until the water went down. At last, it did.

Mr. Lee went to his house. His things were wet and muddy. Neighbors gave him some new things to use.

READ & RESPOND   Point of View

Look at the pronoun "our." Does it give you a clue about who is telling the story?

_____

_____

"Thank you!" he said. He was still
worried. What if the water came back?
"Can we have a party to make
Mr. Lee happy again?" I asked Mom.
"Good idea!" she answered.

READ & RESPOND

Monitor and Clarify

Why is Mr. Lee sad? Reread the text to help you answer.

_____

_____

_____

At the party, Jody and I sang a silly song.
I barked like a dog.

There was a knock at the door. A man gave
Mr. Lee a letter. He read it and smiled.

READ & RESPOND   Point of View

The narrator says, "I barked like a dog." Does this help you know
whether the narrator is a character in the story? Use the illustration to
help you.

_____

_____

Mr. Lee showed us the letter. "I have been offered a new home," he said. "It is up on a hill. I will not have to worry about floods!"

READ & RESPOND

Monitor and Clarify

Why won't Mr. Lee have to worry about floods in his new home?

_____

_____

_____

We were glad. The house was not far away. Mr. Lee would still be our neighbor!

"Come visit me," he said. "You, too, silly dog. You helped me to laugh!"

READ & RESPOND ▶   Point of View

Is the narrator a real dog? Explain how you know.

_____

_____

_____

Reread and Respond

1 **Is Mom a good neighbor? Explain.**

_____

_____

_____

Hint
For a clue, see page 51.

2 **How do Mr. Lee's neighbors help him after the flood?**

_____

_____

_____

Hint
For clues, see pages 52 and 53.

3 **How do you think Mr. Lee feels about his neighbors?**

_____

_____

_____

Hint
For clues, see pages 53 and 56.

Diva
the Dancer

by Duncan Searl

Diva was a dog.
She was also a dancer.
Diva needed a job.
"Maybe I can work at the circus,"
Diva said.
Diva went to the circus. She asked
for a job dancing.

READ & RESPOND

Make and Confirm Predictions

Do you think Diva will find a job at the circus? What do you think she
will do?

_____

_____

The circus people had only one kind of job. "Work up here with us," they said. Diva shook her head. "Those jobs look dangerous! I just want to dance."

READ & RESPOND

Theme

What problem does Diva have? How do you think she will solve it?

_____

_____

_____

Diva went to Officer Lee for a job. "You can help me catch bad guys," said Officer Lee.

"No, thanks," said Diva. "That might scare me. Besides, I want to dance."

READ & RESPOND

Make and Confirm Predictions

What do you think will happen next?

_____

_____

_____

Mr. Ray wanted a nice quiet pet. Diva got the job. Diva was happy. She began to dance. "No dancing!" Mr. Ray said. "I want peace and quiet!" So Diva moved on.

READ & RESPOND

Theme

Do you think Diva is going to give up on her dream? Explain.

_____

_____

_____

Mrs. Bibb wanted a dog for her boys. "I'm great with children," Diva told her.

The Bibb boys weren't great for Diva. They were always screaming. There was too much noise for Diva to dance.

READ & RESPOND   **Make and Confirm Predictions**

Do you think Diva is going to stay with the Bibb boys?

_____

_____

_____

Diva left the Bibbs. Outside, she heard music in the breeze.

Diva followed the music. She came to a house. It was near a park.

READ & RESPOND

Make and Confirm Predictions

What kind of place do you think Diva found? What do you think is going to happen?

_____

_____

The house was a dance school.
"I need a helper," the teacher told Diva.
"Can you dance?"

Diva began to dance. And she's been
dancing ever since.

Theme

**What can you learn from Diva? What lesson do you think the author
wants you to learn?**

_____

_____

Reread and Respond

1 Why did Diva go to the circus?

_____

_____

_____

Hint

For a clue, see page 58.

2 Why did Diva leave the Bibbs?

_____

_____

_____

Hint

For a clue, see page 62.

3 Did Diva get the right job in the end? How do you know?

_____

_____

_____

Hint

For a clue, see page 64.

The **Big** City

by John Berry

Sam looked out the window. Texas was fading away. His dad was reading a paper. His mom was reading a book.

Sam's family was moving to New York City. Sam was sad. He missed Texas already.

READ & RESPOND

Theme

How does Sam feel about moving to New York City?

_____

_____

_____

At last the plane landed. New York City looked very tall. Sam stared. He did not know this city. He did not have friends here. He might have trouble feeling at home.

READ & RESPOND   Theme

Why does Sam think he might have trouble "feeling at home"?

_____

_____

_____

They went to their new home. Sam couldn't sleep that night. He heard horns. He heard sirens. His mom and dad were awake, too.

"What shall we do tomorrow?" said his mom. "Let's plan."

READ & RESPOND   Retell

Why can't Sam and his family sleep?

_____

_____

_____

The next day, they got on the subway. Sam's dad wanted to go to a hardware store. They failed to get there. They were on the wrong subway. "Next stop, Yankee Stadium," said a voice.

"The baseball stadium?" said Sam. "Wow!"

READ & RESPOND　　　　　　　　　　　Theme

Is Sam excited about the baseball stadium? How do you know?

_____

_____

_____

Sam's mom and dad looked at him. They looked at each other. They smiled.

"Shall we go to the game?" asked his mom.

"Yes!" said Sam.

His dad agreed. They bought tickets. It was a great game. It was a great day.

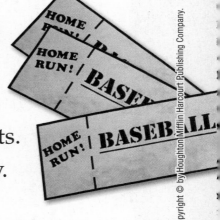

READ & RESPOND

Theme

How do you think Sam feels about New York City now?

_____

_____

_____

They took a subway the next day, too. Sam's mom wanted to shop for curtains. They got on the wrong subway again.

They looked at the map. A polite man helped. "Are you new here?" he said. "You're near a good museum. You should go there."

READ & RESPOND

Retell

What has happened in the story so far?

_____

_____

_____

Sam and his family found the museum. They saw a blue whale. They saw rocks and gems. They saw bugs and snakes.

They walked into a big room. Sam stared. Dinosaurs! "Wow," said Sam. "New York isn't so bad after all!"

READ & RESPOND

What did Sam learn by the end of the story? Does that help you understand the theme of the story?

_____

_____

Reread and Respond

1 **Retell the story in your own words.**

_____

_____

_____

Hint

For help, reread
the story.

2 **How does Sam's opinion of New York change?**

_____

_____

_____

Hint

For clues, see pages
67, 70, and 72.

3 **Is "The Big City" a good title for the story? Explain.**

_____

_____

_____

Hint

There are clues on
almost every page!

Tortoise Gets a Home

by Jake Harris

Forest loved the animals. She gave each one a home.

Lizard got a rock home. Crab got a hole in the sand. Forest forgot all about Tortoise.

READ & RESPOND   Story Structure

What does Forest do?

_____

_____

_____

Snake curled up under leaves. Owl sat in a hole in a tree.

The animals thanked Forest. They were all happy. All but Tortoise! Tortoise was sad.

READ & RESPOND   Main Ideas and Details

Why did the animals thank Forest?

_____

_____

_____

One night, a storm came. Tortoise had no home. He needed to find one. He needed to stay warm and dry.

Tortoise saw a hole in some rocks. Lizard looked out. "Sorry, my house is too small for you," she said.

READ & RESPOND   Story Structure

What problem does Tortoise have?

_____

_____

_____

Tortoise walked toward a hole in the sand. Crab popped his head out.

Tortoise tried to crawl under some leaves. "I'm under here!" said Snake.

READ & RESPOND

Story Structure

How does Tortoise try to solve his problem?

_____

_____

_____

Tortoise went in the direction of a tall tree. Owl hooted at him to go away. The tree was the right height for Owl. It was too tall for Tortoise.

Tortoise did not want to be in the rain. Then he found a broken coconut shell.

READ & RESPOND

Story Structure

Why does Owl tell Tortoise to go away?

_____

_____

_____

Tortoise crawled under the shell. He pulled in his legs. He pulled in his neck. It was just big enough to cover him. Tortoise was warm and dry.

In the morning, the rain had gone. Tortoise came out from his shell. Forest saw him.

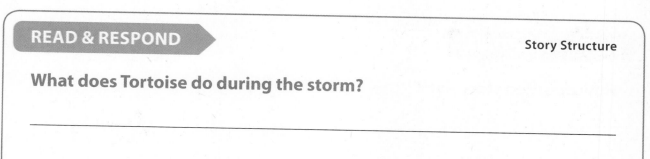

READ & RESPOND

Story Structure

What does Tortoise do during the storm?

_____

_____

_____

"Tortoise!" said Forest. "I am sorry. I forgot to give you a home. I see you found one. This shell will stay on your back. Your home will always be with you."

Today, all tortoises have shells.

READ & RESPOND Story Structure

How does the story end?

_____

_____

_____

Reread and Respond

1 **How does Tortoise feel at the beginning of the story? Why?**

_____

_____

_____

Hint

For clues, see pages 74 and 75.

2 **Why does Tortoise need a home?**

_____

_____

_____

Hint

See page 76.

3 **How do you think Tortoise feels at the end of the story? Why?**

_____

_____

_____

Hint

For clues, see pages 79 and 80.

The New Playground

by Jason Powe

"I have some wonderful news," says Mrs. Ruiz. "You will help plan the new playground!"

"A new playground?" asks Paul.

"That will be fun!" says Rosa.

READ & RESPOND   Make and Confirm Predictions

Do you think the children will have fun planning the playground? Why do you think so?

_____

_____

Mrs. Ruiz takes the children to her office. Their teacher, Mr. Jones, is there, too. The room is quiet.

"How do we begin?" asks Paul.

READ & RESPOND

Create Mental Images

Are there any describing words on this page? What do they tell you?

_____

_____

_____

"Think about what you like to do outside," says Mrs. Ruiz. "Then talk about your ideas."

"We all have to agree," says Mr. Jones.

READ & RESPOND   Make and Confirm Predictions

Do you think the children will all agree? Explain.

_____

_____

_____

Each child thinks. Rosa loves to swing. Lucy thinks of shooting hoops. Paul dreams of playing in the sand.

They write down their ideas. Then it is time to share.

READ & RESPOND

Create Mental Images

What do you picture in your mind when you read this page?

_____

_____

_____

"I noticed that we don't have swings," says Rosa. "Let's get some!"

"I want a basketball court," says Lucy.

"A sandbox, too!" says Paul.

READ & RESPOND

Make and Confirm Predictions

What do you think the new playground will have?

_____

_____

_____

Mrs. Ruiz listens. "I like those ideas," she says.

It takes time to build the playground. The children dream about what it will look like.

READ & RESPOND

Create Mental Images

Look at the picture on this page. What would you hear, see, or feel if you were on the playground?

_____

_____

At last, the playground is ready. It has a sandbox. It has swings. It even has a hoop! The whole school loves the new playground. The children did a good job.

READ & RESPOND   Make and Confirm Predictions

Think about what you said the playground would have. Was your prediction correct? Explain.

_____

_____

Reread and Respond

1 **What is Mrs. Ruiz's wonderful news?**

_____

_____

_____

Hint

For a clue, see page 82.

2 **Where do the children meet to plan the playground?**

_____

_____

_____

Hint

For a clue, see page 83.

3 **Imagine you are planning a playground. What kinds of things would you like?**

_____

_____

_____

Hint

Think about what you like to do outside.

Kate's Helping Day

by Margaret Maugenest

Kate woke up early. It was a special day. She planned to help people.

Kate had promised to help her mom first. Kate was staring into space when her mom called her.

READ & RESPOND

Author's Purpose

Look at the title. Does it give you any clues about why the author may have written the story?

_____

_____

Kate's mom was wearing a hat and gloves. "Are you really going to help me?" asked Mom.

"Sure," said Kate. "May I wear a hat and gloves, too?"

"Yes," said Mom.

Make Connections

Have you ever helped someone before? How did helping someone else make you feel?

_____

_____

Kate helped out in the garden.
Mom told her all about plants.
Kate had fun.
   "We've worked a long time.
We're done, Kate," said Mom.
"Who will you help next?"

READ & RESPOND

Main Ideas and Details

Why did Kate need to wear a hat and gloves to help her mom?

_____

_____

_____

"I'm helping my friend Carol," said Kate. "We're going to paint her room."

Kate put on some old clothes. Then she walked to Carol's home.

Kate hoped she'd like painting. It was hard but fun. She was not disappointed.

READ & RESPOND

Make Connections

Have you ever helped someone paint a room? How does that help you understand what Kate meant by, "It was hard but fun"?

_____

_____

The friends liked painting the walls.
Paint splashed on their old clothes.
They looked in a mirror. They
chuckled about the paint spills.

READ & RESPOND   Author's Purpose

How has the author kept your attention in the story so far?
How does that help you know the author's purpose?

_____

_____

Next, Kate helped her friend Ramón. She
went to his house. They washed his dad's car.
It was hard work. It was worth it.
Ramón's dad paid them. Each of them
received a few dollars.

READ & RESPOND

Make Connections

What is happening at this part of the story?
Have you ever done anything like this?

_____

_____

That night, Kate was tired but happy.
She thought about the day.

She had learned about plants. She had
made a room pretty. She had earned money.

Kate smiled. She liked helping out.

Make Connections

**Think about the ways Kate helped people in the story. Is there anything
you could do in your community to be like Kate? Explain.**

_____

_____

Reread and Respond

1 **What is Kate thinking about when the story begins?**

_____

_____

_____

Hint

For a clue, see page 90.

2 **Whom does Kate help in the story?**

_____

_____

_____

Hint

There are clues on every page!

3 **Where does Kate go to help those people?**

_____

_____

_____

Hint

For clues, see pages 92, 93, and 95.

The Best Pet

by Judy Rosenbaum

Are you looking for a pet?
A dog is a fine pet. A dog will play with
you. It can be a pal.

You can find a good dog at a pet shelter.
Or a mother dog in your neighborhood
may have a litter of pups.

READ & RESPOND

Ideas and Support

**List one opinion found on this page. Then list two facts the author
gives to support her opinion.**

_____

_____

A dog can be a big job, though. You have to walk it. You must brush its coat. A dog can eat a lot, too.

Dogs won't always do the right thing. Some dogs chew everything. Dogs can be loud. Some dogs like to run off.

Are you sure about a dog?

READ & RESPOND   Ideas and Support

The author says that a dog can be a big job. Is that a fact or an opinion? Explain.

_____

_____

You could get a cat. Cats are fine pets. They love to jump, climb, and play.

A cat can be a big job, though. You must brush its fur. You must feed it. You don't have to walk a cat, but you need to spend time with it.

READ & RESPOND   Ideas and Support

What reasons does the author give to support her opinion that cats can be a big job?

_____

_____

Cats won't always do the right thing. Some cats scratch tables and chairs. Some cats hide and spring out at you. Many cats like to be up at night. So they might make noise while you are trying to sleep.

Are you sure about a cat?

READ & RESPOND   Ideas and Support

What examples does the author give to support her reason that cats won't always do the right thing?

_____

_____

What if you want a quiet pet? Then don't look just at mammals. Think about fish!

Fish make no noise at all. They don't even whisper. They don't get out of the house and run off. They stay in their tank. They don't scratch things. They don't even have paws!

Ideas and Support

List three facts the author gives about fish on this page.

_____

_____

_____

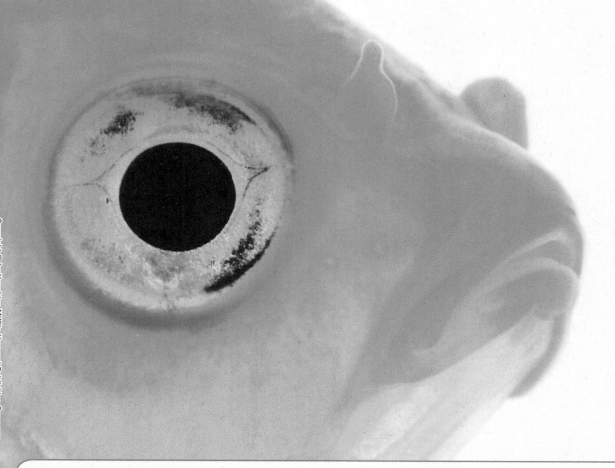

Fish are not hairy like dogs or cats. So you don't have to brush them. They eat only a little bit. They don't need to be walked. You don't need any fish leashes!

Fish are easy to care for. You just have to clean the tank.

READ & RESPOND

Ideas and Support

The author says that fish are easy to care for. Is that a fact or an opinion?

_____

_____

But…
If you want a pet to run around with,
you need to look for something else.

READ & RESPOND   Ideas and Support

Think back on what you read. Which animal do you think is the best pet?
Explain.

_____

_____

Reread and Respond

1 How are fish different from cats and dogs?

_____

_____

_____

Hint

For a clue, look on page 103.

2 What is one reason that dogs are more work than cats?

_____

_____

_____

Hint

Look on pages 99 and 100.

3 Did the author write "The Best Pet" mainly to entertain readers or mainly to give information? How can you tell?

_____

_____

_____

Hint

There are clues on almost every page!

Discovering the Past

by John Berry

What was life like long ago? What did houses look like? What games did kids play? What did they eat?

The answers might be under your feet.

READ & RESPOND

Evaluate and Synthesize

What are you thinking after reading the first page?

_____

_____

_____

Things were left in the dirt. Time passed. Then people discovered the things. People found old coins. They found toys. They found old tools.

These old things are clues. They tell us about the past.

READ & RESPOND   Evaluate and Synthesize

What do you think is the most important detail on this page? How do you know it is the most important?

_____

_____

Some people study the past. It's a fun job. They dig in the dirt.

They find old coins. They find pots. They find tools. These things tell a story. It's a story of the past.

READ & RESPOND   Ideas and Support

The author says that studying the past is a fun job. Is that a fact or an opinion?

_____

_____

The diggers make a map. The map shows the exact places where people find things.

A coin may be deep in the dirt. The map shows where. A pot may be next to a wall. The map shows where.

Evaluate and Synthesize

What do you learn about how people study the past on this page? How does this knowledge change your thinking?

_____

_____

Scientists remove dirt. They study each item. They think about where it was found.

A toy was deep in the dirt. Another toy was near the top. The diggers may think the first toy is older.

READ & RESPOND   Evaluate and Synthesize

Do you find any details on this page interesting? Are these details needed to understand the topic?

_____

_____

People learn from what they find. They thought a pot was for water. It looked like a water pot.

Then they looked closer. They found oil inside the pot. They found bits of food. They were amazed. The pot was for cooking!

Ideas and Support

Look at the sentence: "The pot was for cooking!" Is that a fact or an opinion? How do you know?

_____

_____

You don't have to dig. You can see old things at a museum. You can look at tools. You can look at coins. You can look at toys.
They will tell you about life long ago. Learning about the past is fun.

Ideas and Support

The author says that learning about the past is fun.
Is that a fact or an opinion? Explain.

_____

_____

Reread and Respond

1 **What can you see at a museum?**

_____

_____

_____

Hint

For a clue, see page 270.

2 **Sometimes scientists change their minds about old things. Why?**

_____

_____

_____

Hint

For a clue, see page 111.

3 **Do you think digging for old things would be a fun job? Explain.**

_____

_____

_____

Hint

Think about what diggers do and what they discover.

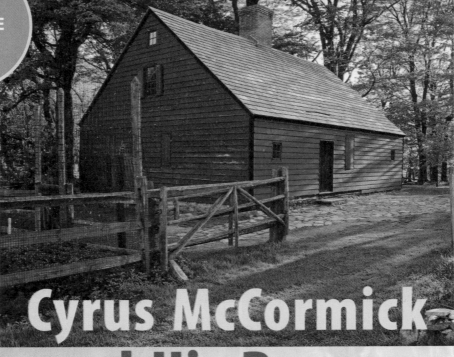

Cyrus McCormick and His Reaper

by John Berry

A Boy Who Made Things

Cyrus McCormick was born in 1809. He lived on a farm. He liked to make things.

Cyrus had a dream. He wanted to be an inventor. He made a new tool when he was fifteen. He used it to carry grain.

READ & RESPOND   Text Organization

What important events does the author talk about on this page? List them in the order they happened.

_____

_____

A Good Idea

Farmers cut grain by hand. They used a big blade. It was hard work.

Cyrus's dad wanted to cut grain faster. He designed a machine. He made it. It never ran right.

READ & RESPOND

Text Organization

Reread the second paragraph. Identify one cause and one effect in this paragraph.

_____

_____

Cyrus's Reaper

Cyrus wanted to try. He made a new machine. It cut grain fast. It would help farmers cut more. It was called a reaper.

He worked on the machine for ten years. He wanted to make it better. He wanted to achieve his goal.

READ & RESPOND   **Main Ideas and Details**

Why did Cyrus work on his machine for ten years?

_____

_____

_____

At last, Cyrus got a good result. The reaper worked better. It had an extra blade. It could cut grain in the rain.

Another man made a reaper. He wanted to have a contest. Whose reaper would work best?

READING & RESPOND

READ & RESPOND

Summarize

Summarize the text so far. Use details in the text to help you.

_____

_____

_____

Battle of the Reapers

The day of the contest was rainy. The other reaper jammed. Cyrus's reaper did not. It cut a lot of grain.

People wanted to buy Cyrus's reaper. He sold twenty-nine machines that year.

READ & RESPOND

Text Organization

What event led to people buying Cyrus's reaper?

_____

_____

_____

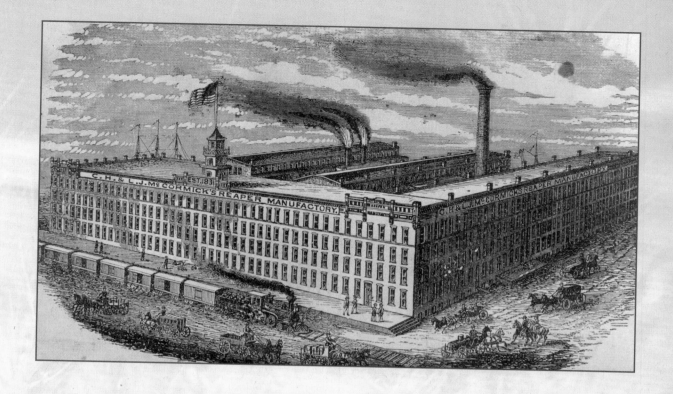

A New Place to Work

Cyrus made reapers on his farm. Many farmers wanted them. Cyrus needed more space.

He moved to Chicago. Workers in his factory made reapers fast. Cyrus sold thousands of machines each year.

READ & RESPOND

Text Organization

Reread the headings on each page. Do they help tell you how the author organized the text?

_____

_____

Success

The reaper was a success. Cyrus was famous all over the world.

He went to London in 1851. He got a medal for his work. His remarkable machine changed farming forever.

READ & RESPOND

Summarize the text in your own words. Think about the most important ideas in the text to help you.

_____

_____

Reread and Respond

1 **How did Cyrus's reaper change farm work?**

_____

_____

_____

Hint

For clues, see pages 116 and 117.

2 **How did Cyrus improve his machine?**

_____

_____

_____

Hint

For a clue, see page 117.

3 **Why did Cyrus move his work to a factory?**

_____

_____

_____

Hint

For a clue, see page 119.

At the Beach

by John Berry

Max collects shells. He knows all about them. He says that millions of animals have shells.

He takes me to the beach. Max is excited. He wants to find a conch shell.

READ & RESPOND

Make Inferences

Why is Max excited to go to the beach?

Max is excited to go to the beach because he wants to find a conch shell.

We get to the beach. Max gets upset.
He finds trash in the sand.

"This is disgusting!" he says. "People
should not litter."

I agree.

READ & RESPOND

Point of View

What pronouns do you see on the first two pages? What do they help
you understand about the point of view?

I see the pronouns he
and we. The story is writeed
in first point of veiw.

123

We look for shells. First we find rocks.
Then we find sticks. At last we find shells.

"Look at this one," I say.

"I have one like that,"

Max says. "See?"

READ & RESPOND

Point of View

Is the narrator a character in the story? What clues in the text help you to know?

Yes, the narrator is a character in the story

He pulls a shell from his bag. It is the same. I toss my shell into the sea.

"Hey! A crab!" I say.

"It has two claws," Max says. "The big one is strong. The small one is weaker."

READ & RESPOND

Make Inferences

Why did the narrator toss his shell into the sea?

The narrator toss his shell into the sea because it's the same one he has.

"There's another crab," I say. "It looks funny."

"That's a hermit crab," says Max. "They find shells to live in. This crab doesn't have a shell."

"You can give him a shell," I say.

READ & RESPOND

Make Inferences

Why does the narrator say that the crab on this page looks funny?

_____

_____

_____

"Hermit crabs live in snail shells," says Max. "I have only one snail shell."

"Well, you have two choices," I say. "You can give the crab a home or keep the shell."

READ & RESPOND

Make Inferences

How does Max feel at this part in the text? How do you know?

_____

_____

_____

I walk away. I look back. Max puts the shell on the sand. The crab goes in. Max looks happy.

I'm happy, too.

READ & RESPOND Point of View

Is this story told in first-person or third-person point of view? How do you know?

_____

_____

Reread and Respond

1 Look at page 123. Write one sentence that is an opinion.

_____

_____

_____

Hint

Remember that an opinion shows what someone thinks or feels.

2 Write one fact that Max tells about shells.

_____

_____

_____

Hint

For clues, see pages 122, 126, and 127.

3 If you were Max, which choice would you have made?

_____

_____

_____

Hint

Think about Max's choices. Think about what Max wants.

Growing Sprouts

by Mia Lewis

Do you eat sprouts? Maybe you eat them on sandwiches. Maybe you eat them in salads. They are used in cooked food, too.

READ & RESPOND

Evaluate

Read the title. What is the topic of the text?

_____

_____

_____

You can buy different kinds of sprouts at a store. Some are mild. Others are spicy. They taste different because they are grown from different kinds of seeds.

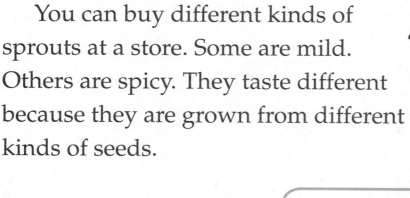

alfalfa sprouts

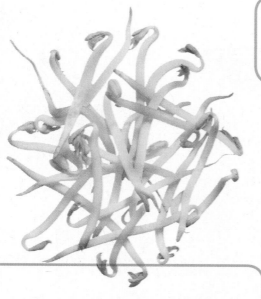

mung bean sprouts

radish sprouts

READ & RESPOND

Text and Graphic Features

How do the captions help you understand the pictures?
How do the pictures connect to the topic of the text?

_____

_____

Lots of seeds and some types of grain can be grown into sprouts. For example, radish seeds, broccoli seeds, and grains of wheat make tasty sprouts.

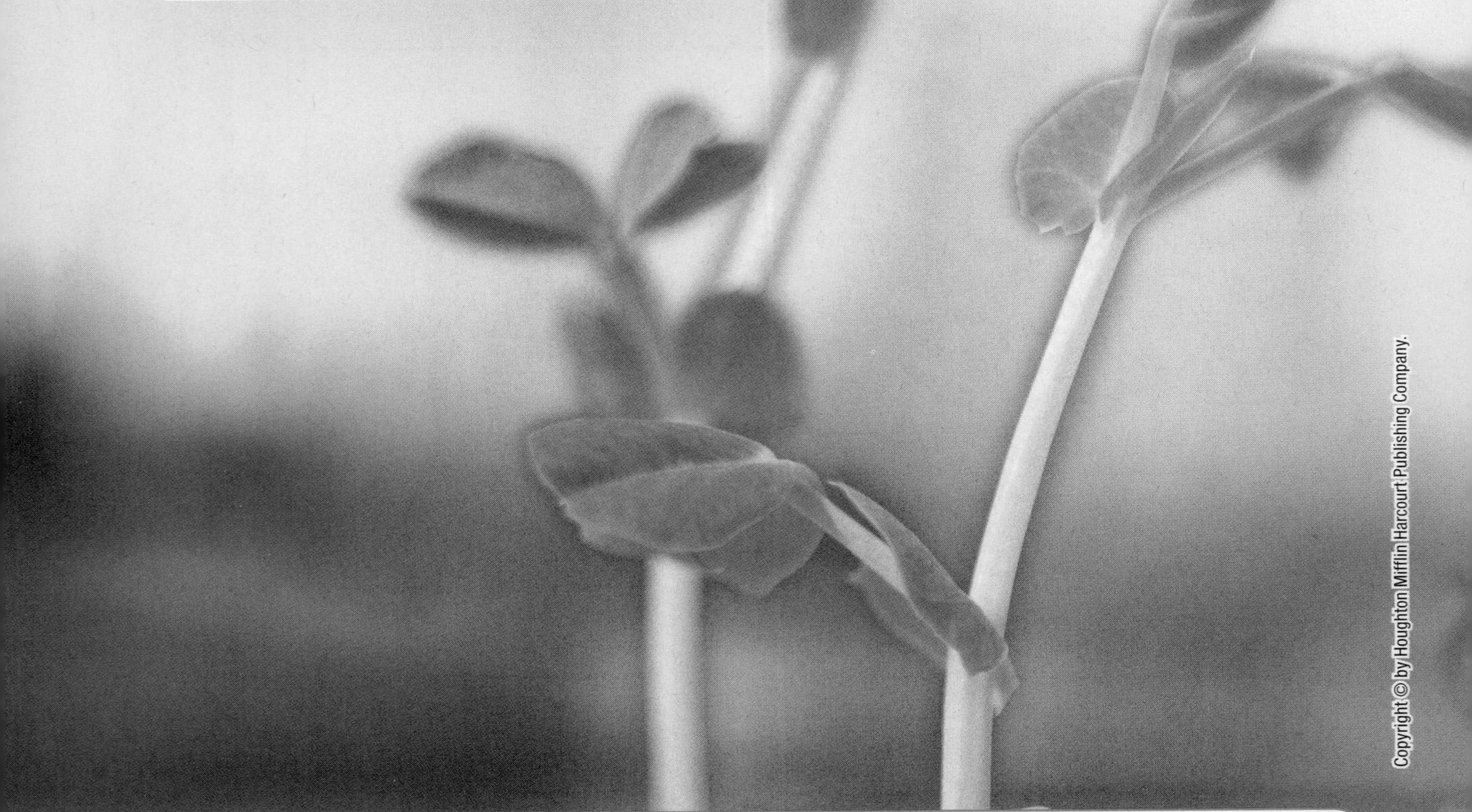

READ & RESPOND **Evaluate**

What details on this page help you understand the topic of the text?

____

____

____

Perhaps the best thing
about sprouts is how easy they
are to grow. You can grow
them at home.

READ & RESPOND

Evaluate

**Why does the author point out that growing sprouts is easy?
Is this idea important?**

_____

_____

All you need is a cup and some seeds.
Put the seeds in the cup, and add water.
Soak them overnight.

READ & RESPOND

Text and Graphic Features

Look at the photograph. What can you learn about sprouts
from this picture?

_____

_____

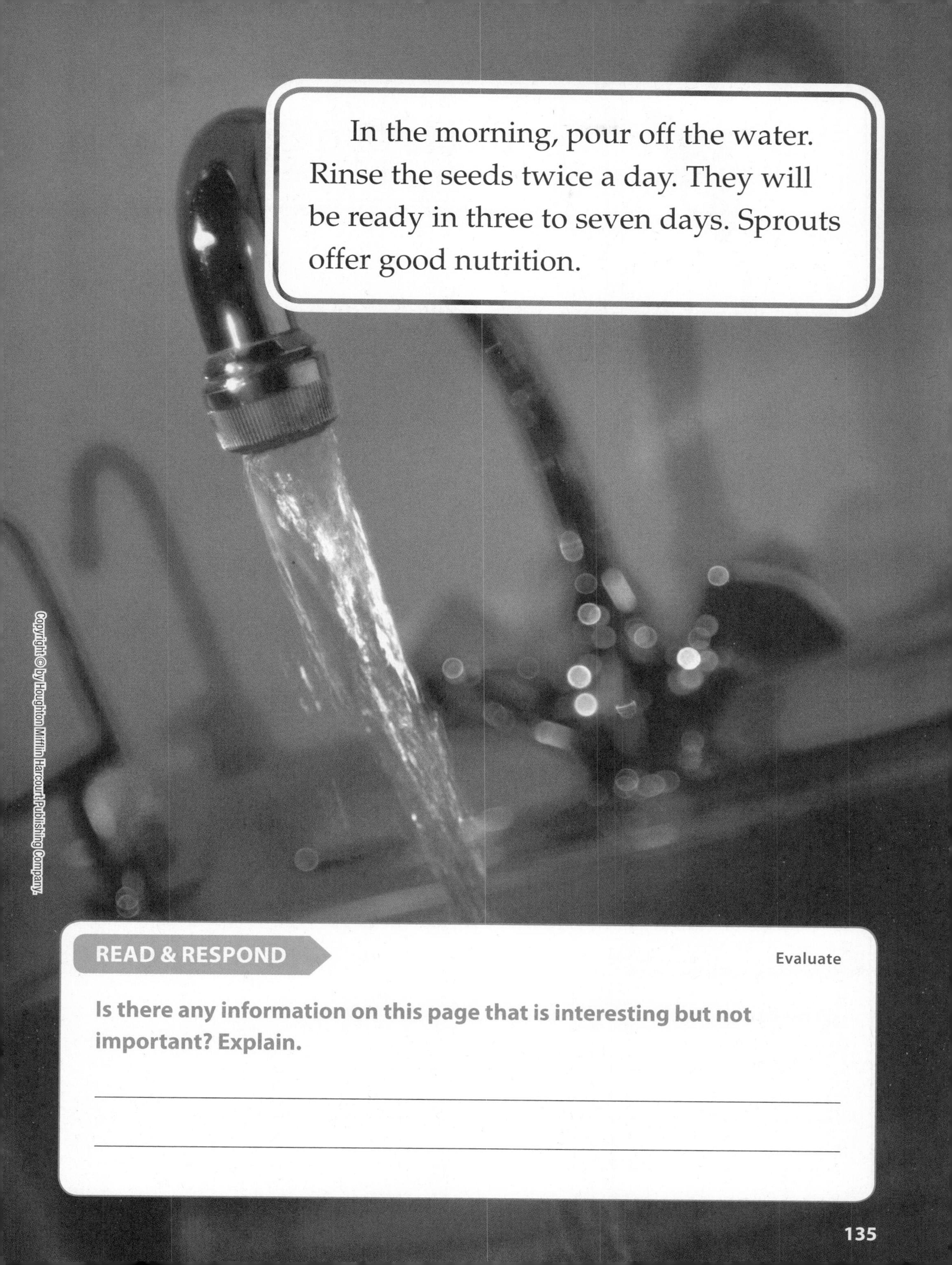

In the morning, pour off the water. Rinse the seeds twice a day. They will be ready in three to seven days. Sprouts offer good nutrition.

READ & RESPOND

Evaluate

Is there any information on this page that is interesting but not important? Explain.

_____

_____

Parts of a Sprout

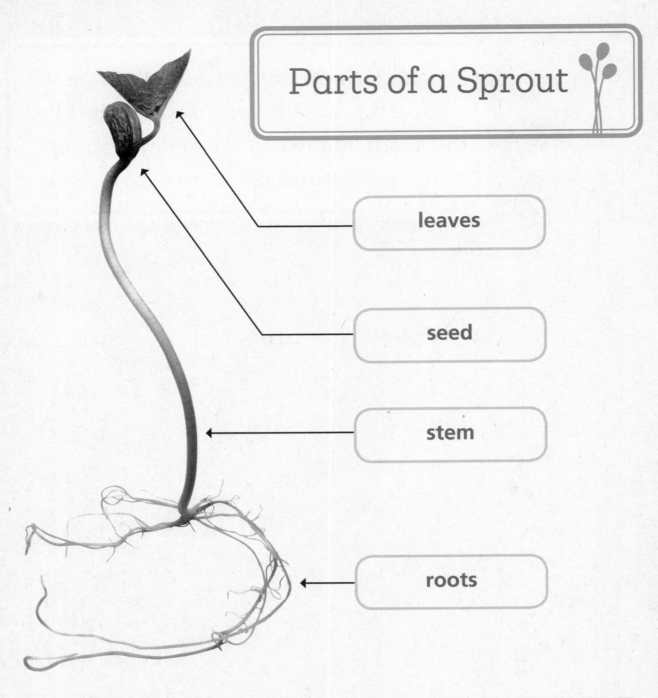

leaves

seed

stem

roots

READ & RESPOND

Text and Graphic Features

Write the parts of a sprout. Use the diagram to help you.

_____

_____

_____

Reread and Respond

1 **What do you need to grow sprouts?**

_____

_____

_____

Hint

For clues, see pages 132 and 134.

2 **How long does it take to grow sprouts?**

_____

_____

_____

Hint

For a clue, see page 135.

3 **Why is it a good idea to grow sprouts?**

_____

_____

_____

Hint

For clues, look on pages 132, 133, and 135.

The Contest

by Mia Lewis

Sun and Wind were talking.

"I'm stronger than you," said Wind. "I can blow a ship across the sea. I can bend a tree to the ground."

"I'm stronger!" said Sun. "I light the day. I can dry up that stream!"

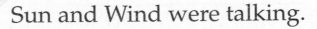

READ & RESPOND   Ask and Answer Questions

Read the title. Do you have any questions about what this story might be about? How can you answer your questions?

_____

_____

Sun saw a man on the road.

"That man is wearing a coat," said Sun. "We will have a contest. If you can make the man take off his coat, you are stronger. If I can make him take it off, I am stronger. You go first!"

Ask and Answer Questions

Does the information on this page answer your question about what the story is about? Explain.

_____

_____

Wind agreed. He wasted no time. He blew a swift breeze at the man. The traveler did not notice.

Wind blew a stronger gust. The man held onto his hat. He kept walking.

READ & RESPOND

Ask and Answer Questions

Do you understand what Wind is doing at this part in the story? What can you do to help you understand?

_____

_____

Now Wind blew a real storm! The trees shook! Leaves were flung into the air.

Wind blew as hard as he could. The man only pulled his coat more tightly around himself.

Ask and Answer Questions

Why did the man pull his coat tighter? What clues in the text can help you answer the question?

_____

_____

At last Wind gave up. "You try," he said to Sun. "Good luck!"

Sun smiled. He shone a little ray. The man kept on walking.

"You see," said Wind. "Neither of us can get him to take off his coat."

READ & RESPOND   Ask and Answer Questions

Write one question you have about what is happening in the text.

_____

_____

_____

Sun was not finished. He shone another ray on the man. He beat down hot and steady.

The man began to sweat. He took off his hat. He opened his coat. After a while, he took his coat all the way off.

READ & RESPOND

Ask and Answer Questions

Do you understand how Sun got the man to take off his coat? What can help you understand?

_____

_____

Wind clapped. Sun bowed. The man walked peacefully down the road in his T-shirt.

• • • • • • • •

The story has a moral. Persuade gently. It works better than force.

READ & RESPOND　　　　　　　　Ask and Answer Questions

Write one question you have now that you have finished reading.

_____

_____

_____

Reread and Respond

1 **Who won the contest? How did he win?**

_____

_____

_____

Hint

For a clue, see
page 143 and 144.

2 **Why does the man remove his hat?**

_____

_____

_____

Hint

For a clue, see
page 143.

3 **Write the moral of the story in your own words.**

_____

_____

_____

Hint

Read the moral on
page 144.

Game Time!

by John Berry

What games do you play? Do you play with a ball? Do you play board games?

Kids play all over the world. Every culture has its own games. There are many ways to have fun!

READ & RESPOND   Synthesize

What do you think is the big idea of this text? What clues on this page help you to know?

_____

_____

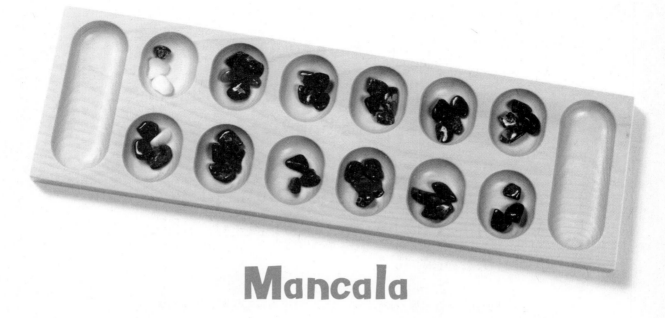

Mancala

Mancala is a counting game. It was first played in Africa. You can play with seeds. You can play with stones.

Players pick up the stones. They drop them into the bins. It seems easy, but it is hard to play well!

READ & RESPOND   Ideas and Support

Reread the last sentence on this page. Is this a fact or an opinion? How do you know?

_____

_____

Pachisi

Pachisi comes from India. Players move pieces on a board. Each player wants to get to the middle first.

Long ago, rulers in India played Pachisi. Today, people play in other countries, too.

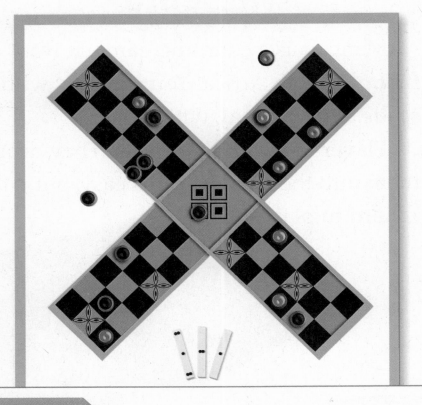

READ & RESPOND   Synthesize

What information on this page supports the big idea?

_____

_____

_____

Games with String

The Inuit are native people. They are from North America. People in the Inuit community learn to make string shapes. It is their tradition.

Children all over play games with string. Cat's cradle is one string game.

READ & RESPOND   Ideas and Support

What examples does the author give to support his claim that every culture has its own games? Explain.

_____

_____

Soccer

People all over the world play soccer. More people play soccer than any other game!

Players run. They kick the ball. They cannot touch it with their hands. Players often wear uniforms.

READ & RESPOND   Ideas and Support

The author says that more people play soccer than any other game. Is this a fact or an opinion? How do you know?

_____

_____

A Battle Game

A game was invented in China. It is hundreds of years old. It is played with stones on a board. The game is called Go.

The game is a battle. Players trap each other's stones. They must plan well. It takes skill to win!

READ & RESPOND

Ideas and Support

Reread the last sentence on this page. Is this a fact or an opinion? How do you know?

_____

_____

Marbles

Long ago, children in Egypt played a game with marbles. Kids still play marbles today. Kids collect marbles, too.

Marbles come in many colors. Some special marbles are called cat's eyes. They sparkle like the eyes of a cat.

READ & RESPOND   Synthesize

Did you learn anything new about this topic after reading? Explain.

_____

_____

_____

Reread and Respond

1 What is the most popular game in the world?

_____

_____

_____

Hint

For a hint, see page 150.

2 How are Go and Pachisi alike?

_____

_____

_____

Hint

For hints, see pages 148 and 151.

3 Name a big idea that the text tells about games.

_____

_____

_____

Hint

For clues, see page 146.

I Made It Myself

by Margaret Maugenest

My grandma and I take a walk. We pass a shop window. I point to a red scarf.

"That's pretty," I say.

"You can knit a scarf like this," says Ama. "I'll show you how, Rosie."

"Really?" I ask.

READ & RESPOND

Make Inferences

Does Ama know how to knit? How do you know?

_____

_____

_____

We go to Ama's house. Ama gets a box.
Inside are balls of white yarn.

"You can use this to make a scarf,"
she says.

"This yarn is white," I say.
"I want a red scarf."

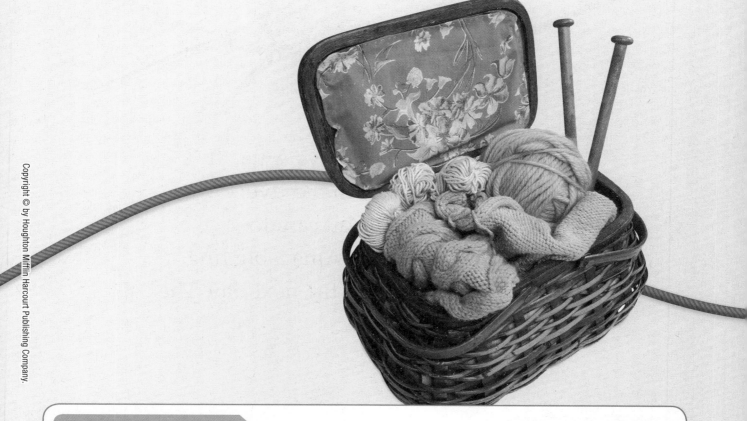

READ & RESPOND

Monitor and Clarify

How is Rosie going to make a scarf?

_____

_____

_____

"I can make it red," says Ama. "I know how. I'll soak it in red dye."

"You're so smart. You can do anything!" I say. I give Ama a big hug.

I go to Ama's house the next day. The wool is red.

READ & RESPOND ➤
Make Inferences

How did the wool become red? How do you know?

_____

_____

_____

"Let's knit," Ama says.

She shows me how to hold the knitting needles. "Bring the yarn under first. Then bring it over the needle," she says.

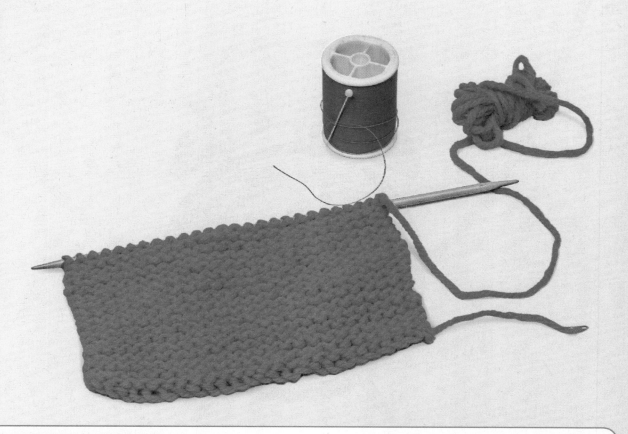

READ & RESPOND

Monitor and Clarify

Do you know someone who can knit or crochet? How does that help you understand this part of the story?

_____

_____

I make my first stitch. I make another stitch. I finish my first row. Then I knit another row.

"I don't see much scarf yet," I say.

"It takes time," says Ama.

"It sure does!" I say.

READ & RESPOND

Make Inferences

Do you think Ama is patient? Do you think Rosie is patient? Explain.

_____

_____

_____

I knit every day. My cat Ruby likes to watch. I cut some strands of yarn. She plays with them.

My scarf starts to get long. I keep knitting. My scarf is getting longer!

READ & RESPOND

Make Inferences

How can you tell Rosie likes to knit?

_____

_____

_____

I knit for many weeks.

At last, my scarf is done. Ama helps me finish it. I put it around my neck.

"Thank you. It is beautiful," I say.

"I'm proud of you," says Ama. "You duplicated the scarf! You're a real knitter!"

READ & RESPOND

Make Inferences

Do you think Rosie will knit something else? Explain.

_____

_____

_____

Reread and Respond

1 How can you tell that Ama is a good teacher?

_____

_____

_____

Hint

For a clue, see page 160.

2 Does it take Rosie a long time to knit her scarf? How do you know?

_____

_____

_____

Hint

For clues, see pages 158, 159, and 160.

3 How can you tell that Rosie and Ama get along well?

_____

_____

_____

Hint

Clues are on almost every page!

★True★Heroes★

by Karen Bischoff

Josh loved baseball. The Stars were his favorite team. The player Rick Callan was his hero. Josh had never been to a game. He had seen games only on TV.

READ & RESPOND　　　　　　　　　　　　　　　Setting

Where does this part of the story take place? How do you know?

_____

_____

_____

One day, Josh's dad came home
smiling. "My boss had extra tickets to the
game," he said. "He gave them to me."
"Wow!" shouted Josh. He was happy.

READ & RESPOND

Create Mental Images

What words on this page help you picture how Josh and his dad feel?

_____

_____

_____

The game was great. Josh could see all the players. He cheered a lot.

He loved to watch Rick Callan. He played like a hero. He hit a home run. The final score was 7 to 4. The Stars won.

READ & RESPOND

Create Mental Images

Think about a time you've been to a game. List three things you think Josh and his dad might have heard, smelled, or tasted at the game.

_____

_____

On the way to the car, Josh stopped. He saw Rick Callan! Josh hurried over to him. "Will you sign my program?" he asked.

"Sorry. I'm in a rush," Rick Callan said. He kept walking.

READ & RESPOND   Setting

Where are Josh and his dad now? How do you know?

_____

_____

_____

Josh was upset. Rick Callan had not been nice to him. Josh said, "I thought he was a hero. I was wrong."

"Never mind," Dad said. "I can take you to a real hero."

READ & RESPOND

Create Mental Images

List three things you might see, hear, taste, or smell if you were in the car with Josh and his dad.

_____

_____

Josh's dad took him to a house. "Josh, this is Mrs. Evans. I had a secret. She helped me with it," Dad said.

"What was the secret?" Josh asked.

"I couldn't read," said Dad.

READ & RESPOND

Setting

Has the setting of the story changed? What clues in the text help you to know?

_____

_____

"Mrs. Evans taught me to read," Dad said. "She's my hero. A hero teaches you something."

"Your dad is my hero," said Mrs. Evans. "He worked hard to learn."

Josh smiled. "I have two new heroes now," he said.

READ & RESPOND Main Ideas and Details

What does Josh mean when he says he has two new heroes?

_____

_____

_____

Reread and Respond

1 List at least three settings from the story.

_____

_____

_____

Hint

Look at the pictures to help you.

2 When does Josh meet Rick Callan?

_____

_____

_____

Hint

For clues, see pages 164 and 165.

3 Who are Josh's heroes at the end of the story?

_____

_____

_____

Hint

For a clue, see page 168.

Keeping Safe in a
Storm

by Carol Alexander

Big storms can be scary. Strong winds are loud. They shake things. Pounding rain falls.

Storms can cause harm. Still, you can prepare. You can take steps to keep safe.

READ & RESPOND

Evaluate

Look at the title. Whom or what do you think this text will be about?

I think the text will be about how to keep safe in a storm.

Planning

You should plan ahead. Find safe places at home. They should be away from windows and doors.

You may need supplies. You can put water in bottles. You can freeze food. Make sure you have candles, too.

READ & RESPOND ▶   **Text Organization**

What is the first step in keeping safe in a storm? How do you know?

The first step is find a
safe place at home. I
_____

Before a Storm

You can learn about a storm that is coming. Just listen to the TV or radio. Experts watch the path of storms. News reporters warn people about bad storms.

Some storms are very strong. It may not be safe to stay at home. You may have to go to a safer place.

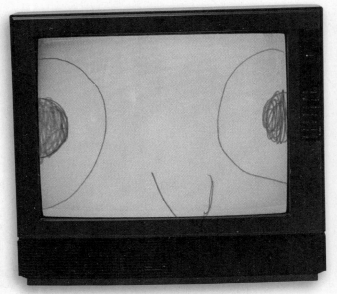

Evaluate

What do you think is the most important idea on this page?

I think is the most important Idea on this page is you may need to go to a safer place during a storm.

You can prevent problems at home.
Bring toys and pets inside. Put garbage
cans where wind can't tip them over.

Wind can damage windows. Some
people tape windows. Tape makes
them stronger.

READ & RESPOND

Text Organization

List two things that can happen if the wind blows too hard.

1. One thing is a lot of things can fly away.
2. It can damage windows.

During a Storm

The storm hits! You should not go outside. Find a safe place inside.

You can play games. Don't play games that use electricity. Things that use electricity can be dangerous in storms. Beware of computers. Do not talk on the phone.

READ & RESPOND   Text Organization

What is the heading on this page? What does it tell you?

The heading on this page is durling a storm. It tells me what todo durling a storm.

174

After a Storm

Listen to the news. Reporters will tell you when it is safe to go outside.

You must still be careful. Stay away from damaged trees. Ask a grownup where you can play.

Isn't it good to be outside again?

READ & RESPOND

Text Organization

What is the last thing the author explains in the text?

The last thing the author explains in the text is what too when when the storm ends.

Kinds of Storms

A **blizzard** is a bad winter storm. It has big winds. It has lots of snow.

A **tornado** is a tube of wind. It can pick up a house!

A **hurricane** is a storm from the sea. It has big winds and waves. It can cause bad floods.

READ & RESPOND   Evaluate

Do you think the information on this page is interesting or important? Explain.

_____

_____

Reread and Respond

1. **What are two things you can do to plan ahead for storms?**

   Hint
   For clues, look on page 171.

   Find safe places and make sure you have candles.

2. **How can you protect your home?**

   Hint
   For clues, look on page 173.

   By taping your windows so the wind won't damage your windows.

3. **How can you tell when it is safe to go outside after a storm?**

   Hint
   For a clue, look on page 175.

   Reporters will tell you when it is safe to go outside.

Fluff, Gus, and Bob

by Richard Stull

Fluff, Gus, and Bob lived together in a house. Fluff was an orange cat. Gus was gray. Bob was black and white.

READ & RESPOND
Characters

Describe one of the characters. Use the story to help you.

_____

_____

_____

"Let's search the cupboard," said Fluff. "We'll find something to eat there." Fluff ran to the cupboard. She found cans of cat food.

"We can't open the cans," said Gus and Bob.

READ & RESPOND

Characters

How do the cats feel at this part of the story?

_____

_____

_____

179

"I know what to do," said Fluff. "Let's ask Jimmy to help."

"Jimmy doesn't know we can talk," said Gus and Bob. "He might find it odd that cats can talk."

Characters

Which cat seems to make most decisions?

_____

_____

_____

Just then, Jimmy came home from school. First he petted the cats. Then he turned on the TV to watch cartoons.

Fluff, Gus, and Bob all spoke at once. "Hey, Jimmy," they said. "We want something to eat."

READ & RESPOND

Characters

What is the first thing Jimmy does when he gets home from school?

_____

_____

_____

Jimmy jumped up from his chair. "Who said that?" he asked.

"We did," said the cats. "We're sorry if we startled you."

"You see, we're hungry," said Fluff.

"We're starving," said Gus and Bob.

READ & RESPOND

Characters

Why is Jimmy surprised?

_____

_____

_____

"Cats can't talk!" said Jimmy.

"Of course we can talk," said Fluff.

"Do you think we just sleep all day?" asked Gus and Bob.

"Well," said Jimmy. "Now I know that you can talk."

READ & RESPOND   Characters

Which two cats always talk at the same time?

_____

_____

_____

"I'm glad you can talk," said Jimmy. "I've got three new friends."

"Three hungry friends," said the cats.

"Oh," said Jimmy. "I almost forgot." He opened a can of cat food for his grateful friends.

> **READ & RESPOND** Characters
>
> Is Jimmy a good pet owner? Explain.
>
> _____
>
> _____
>
> _____

Reread and Respond

1 **Why do the cats talk to Jimmy?**

Hint
For a clue, see page 181.

_____

_____

_____

2 **Fluff finds food in the cupboard. Why don't the cats eat it?**

Hint
For a clue, see page 179.

_____

_____

_____

3 **Jimmy is a kind person. How do you know?**

Hint
For clues, see pages 181 and 184.

_____

_____

_____

Sue and the Tired Wolf

by John Berry

Sue lived in a blue house with her mom and dad. The house had a big yard. It was next to a forest.

Sue studied music. She played songs on her flute every day.

READ & RESPOND

Story Structure

Who is the main character in the story?

_____

_____

_____

One day, Sue's mom and dad wanted some quiet. "Too much noise!" they said.

"I will go outside, then," said Sue. Her mom told her to play in the yard. She should not go in the woods. Sue agreed.

She sat in a leaf pile. She played her flute loudly.

Story Structure

What is the problem in the story? What does Sue decide to do?

_____

_____

_____

Sue got bored. She wanted to explore the woods. She told herself she would go for just a bit. She walked into the forest. The trees were tall. The forest was dark. Sue kept playing her flute. She liked the sound of her flute in the forest.

READ & RESPOND

Story Structure

Why does Sue walk into the forest?

_____

_____

_____

All of a sudden, Sue stopped playing.
A wolf was sitting on a rock. He was
gazing at her.

"You surprised me!" Sue said. She
was scared. She tried to smile.

"I like the sound of your flute. I think
this forest is too quiet," said the wolf.

READ & RESPOND

Story Structure

What does Sue see in the forest? Do you think that is a problem for Sue? Explain.

_____

_____

The wolf was tired and sore. He said, "I have been hunting all day. I want to rest and listen to music."

Sue played her flute. The wolf grew sleepy. His eyelids closed as Sue played.

READ & RESPOND   Story Structure

What is happening at this part of the story?

_____

_____

_____

Sue began to run away, but the wolf woke up. He sprang off the rock. "Why did you stop?" he asked.

"I have to get home," said Sue.

"You can't go! Play more!"

READ & RESPOND

Story Structure

What is Sue's problem now? How do you think she will solve it?

_____

_____

_____

Sue blew a new tune. The wolf grew sleepy again. He started to snore.

Sue walked a few steps. Then she played again. The wolf snored louder. The trick seemed to work!

She used the trick a few more times. At last she was home! Now she knew why she had to stay out of the woods.

READ & RESPOND

Story Structure

How does Sue get away from the wolf?

_____

_____

_____

Reread and Respond

1 Sue's yard is safe to play in. What is the forest like?

_____

_____

_____

Hint

For clues, see pages 188 and 189.

2 What does the wolf think of Sue's music?

_____

_____

_____

Hint

For a clue, see page 189.

3 Do you think Sue will go back to the forest?

_____

_____

_____

Hint

For a clue, see page 192.

Louis Braille

by Karen Bischoff

Louis Braille was born about two hundred years ago. He became blind at the age of three. Louis was unable to see for the rest of his life.

Louis was smart. He tried to do well at school. However, he could not read. He could not write. Louis had to leave school. Still, he wanted to learn.

READ & RESPOND   Text Organization

Whom or what is this text about? What is the first thing the author tells you about Louis Braille?

_____

_____

A Special School

Louis got a lucky break. He joined a special school. It was for children who could not see. He learned a lot there.

Louis was curious. He wanted to learn more. He wanted the knowledge he could get from books.

Copyright © by Houghton Mifflin Harcourt Publishing Company.

READ & RESPOND   Main Ideas and Details

Where did Louis go to school?

_____

_____

_____

Louis Gets an Idea

Louis was blind, but he could feel with his fingers. He had an idea to make writing that people could feel. He thought of letters made of dots. They would be little bumps on the paper.

READ & RESPOND   Text Organization

Tell why Louis wanted to write letters made of dots.

_____

_____

_____

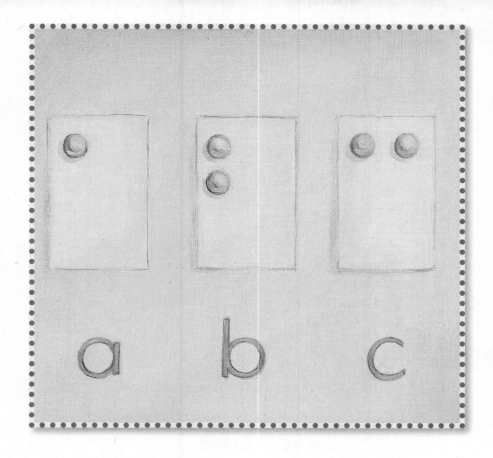

Louis took paper. He made little bumps on it. Each set of bumps was a letter. When he joined the letters, he made words. Louis was writing!

Louis made a motion over the bumps with his fingers. He could feel the bumps. He was reading with his hands!

READ & RESPOND   Text Organization

In order, list the steps Louis took to read with his hands.

_____

_____

_____

Braille

Louis was only 15 years old. He made an alphabet for blind people. That alphabet is now called braille.

His idea let him write. It let other blind people read what he wrote. He started to make books written in braille.

Main Ideas and Details

Who needed Louis's alphabet?

_____

_____

_____

Helping Others

Louis stayed at the school. He became a teacher. He showed children how to read in braille. He showed them how to write in braille.

The children loved Louis. He opened the door to a new world for them.

READ & RESPOND

Text Organization

What happened after Louis finished school?

Braille Today

Today, you can find braille books in stores and in libraries. People all over the world read braille.

Many people cannot see. Thanks to Louis Braille, they can read and write.

READ & RESPOND   **Main Ideas and Details**

Why do people today remember Louis Braille?

_____

_____

_____

Reread and Respond

1 Why do you think the author told you that Louis Braille was blind?

Hint
You must read every page to answer this.

_____

_____

_____

2 What is braille?

Hint
For clues, see pages 198 and 199.

_____

_____

_____

3 Did the author write "Louis Braille" to entertain you or to give you information?

Hint
Did you learn something new?

_____

_____

_____

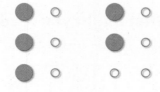

L O U I S   B R A I L L E

♪ Musical Instruments

by Mia Lewis

Music is fun to hear, and even more fun to play! One day you may get to pick an instrument to learn. Read about the different kinds so you can make a good choice.

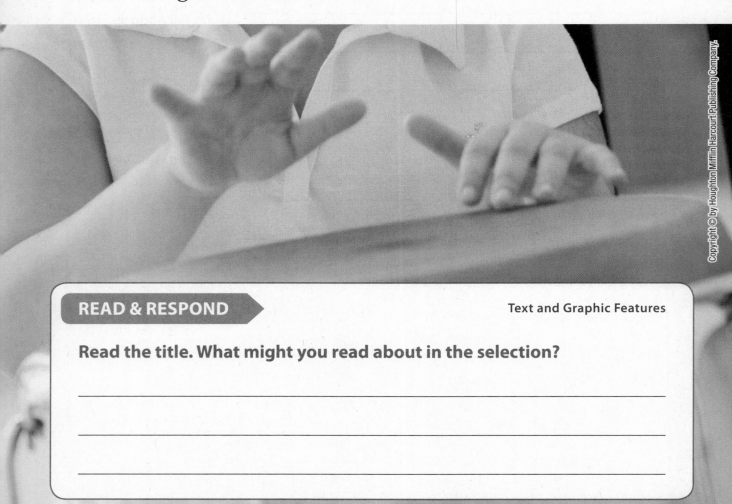

READ & RESPOND

Text and Graphic Features

Read the title. What might you read about in the selection?

_____

_____

_____

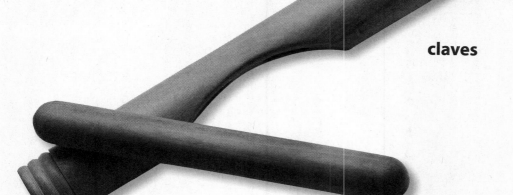

claves

maracas

Percussion Instruments

Do you like to bang and crash? Do you like to rattle and shake? Do you like to bash and boom? If you do, a percussion instrument might be just right for you.

READ & RESPOND

Text and Graphic Features

Look at the illustrations on the page. How do they help you understand what a percussion instrument is?

_____

_____

Wind Instruments

If you blow into it and it makes a noise, it's a wind instrument. A whistle and a kazoo are wind instruments. So are flutes and recorders.

READ & RESPOND   Main Ideas and Details

What creates the sound in a wind instrument?

_____

_____

_____

Brass Instruments

Trumpets, tubas, and trombones are brass instruments—one family of wind instruments. They are good for playing at a high volume. Hear them in a marching band!

tuba

READ & RESPOND

Text and Graphic Features

How does the heading on this page help you to understand what you are reading?

_____

_____

String Instruments

A violin is a string instrument. So is a guitar. A cello is, too. You use a bow or pluck with your fingers to play a tune.

violin

READ & RESPOND

Text and Graphic Features

Does the text tell you what a violin looks like? What features in the text do tell you what a violin looks like?

_____

_____

No Instrument?

Don't like any of these? That's OK. Sing, clap, stamp, or snap. You can be your own instrument. Or grab a pot and a spoon. Get creative. Make your own!

READ & RESPOND

Main Ideas and Details

What does the author say you can do if you don't like any of the instruments?

_____

_____

On Stage

It is fun to see a musical performance. It is even more fun to play in one! Practice hard. Concentrate in music class. You will soon be on stage!

READ & RESPOND

Text and Graphic Features

What kinds of instruments are in the picture on this page?

_____

_____

_____

Reread and Respond

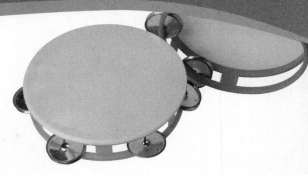

1 Name two wind instruments.

_____

_____

_____

Hint

See pages 204 and
205 for clues.

2 What are two ways string instruments are played?

_____

_____

_____

Hint

See page 206 for
clues.

3 How can a person be a musical instrument?

_____

_____

_____

Hint

See page 207 for
a clue.

Mr. Reed's Last Day

by Claire Daniel

Today is Mr. Reed's last day. He is leaving his job. Mr. Reed is going back to school. He will be training. He will learn to teach computer skills to kids.

READ & RESPOND ▶   Main Ideas and Details

Where is Mr. Reed going?

_____

_____

_____

It is his last day. His students know. They smile a lot. No one says a thing.

Mr. Reed wants to go learn more. It is a sensible thing to do. Still, he is not so happy. He is leaving. He thinks the children do not care.

READ & RESPOND

Main Ideas and Details

Why isn't Mr. Reed happy?

_____

_____

_____

The principal comes to class. She brings
Curt and Gina. They wink at each other.

"Now I need Ann," the principal says.
"Her father is here."

"This is odd," Mr. Reed says. The
children just smile.

READ & RESPOND   Retell

What has happened in the story so far?

_____

_____

_____

All day long, the principal picks up children. Then she brings them back.

Mr. Reed gives the children a test. They do not mind. They smile and smile. Mr. Reed says, "That's odd, too."

READ & RESPOND

Retell

What have the children been doing all day?

_____

_____

_____

Then the principal asks for Ann, Gina, and Curt again. Now Mr. Reed is very confused.

Curt, Ann, and Gina come back. They have food, party hats, and a big box.

"Surprise!" the children yell.

READ & RESPOND   Main Ideas and Details

What do the children have when they come back? Why do they yell?

_____

_____

_____

Ann says, "My dad brought this balloon."

Gina says, "The principal helped us write notes."

Curt says, "We put the notes onto the balloon. They will make you think of us."

READ & RESPOND

Retell

What did the children do for Mr. Reed?

_____

_____

_____

Now Mr. Reed is happy. He says, "This is no ordinary surprise!"

He ties the balloon to his bike. He rides home. The students wave. They will miss him.

READ & RESPOND

Retell

Retell the story in your own words.

_____

_____

_____

Reread and Respond

1 **What is the problem in this story?**

_____

_____

_____

Hint

For a clue, see page 211.

2 **What do the children do on Mr. Reed's last day?**

_____

_____

_____

Hint

For clues, see pages 214, 215, and 216.

3 **How does this story end?**

_____

_____

_____

Hint

For a clue, see page 216.

Joe and Trig and the Baby Turtles

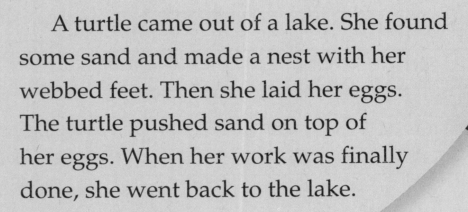

by Karen Bischoff

A turtle came out of a lake. She found some sand and made a nest with her webbed feet. Then she laid her eggs. The turtle pushed sand on top of her eggs. When her work was finally done, she went back to the lake.

READ & RESPOND   Make Inferences

Why does the turtle have webbed feet?

_____

_____

_____

Many days passed. The eggs cracked. One baby turtle was fast. It got out of its shell first. It pushed its way out of the nest. It needed to get to the water. It was not safe on the ground. Birds like to eat baby turtles.

READ & RESPOND

Main Ideas and Details

Why does the turtle need to get to the water?

_____

_____

_____

Close by, Joe was fishing. His Uncle Rob brought him to the lake. Joe had his dog, Trig. Trig was sniffing around the edge of the lake. Trig barked. Joe went over to Trig.

Make Inferences

What makes Joe go to see Trig?

_____

_____

_____

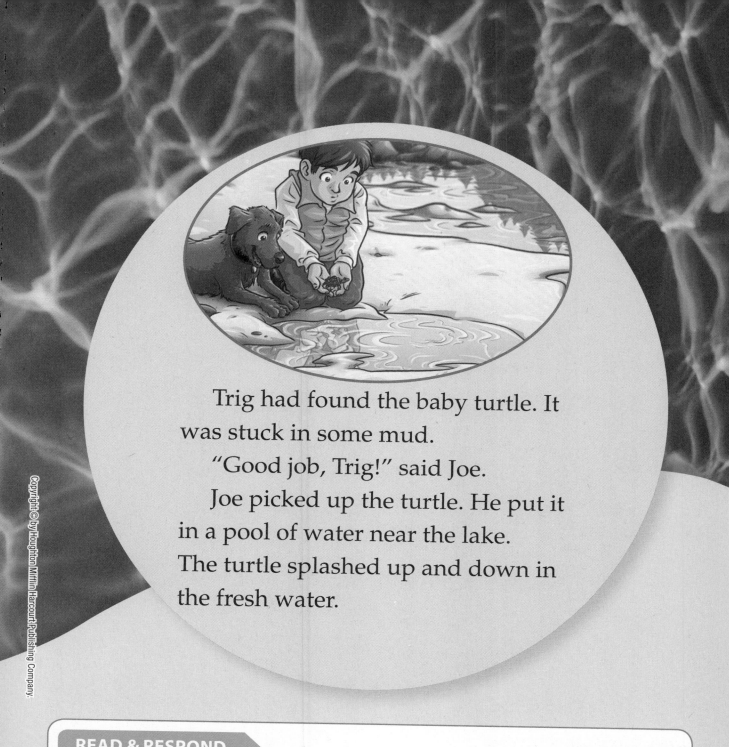

Trig had found the baby turtle. It was stuck in some mud.

"Good job, Trig!" said Joe.

Joe picked up the turtle. He put it in a pool of water near the lake. The turtle splashed up and down in the fresh water.

Make Inferences

Why does the turtle splash in the water?

_____

_____

_____

Joe looked around. "Are there more turtles?" he asked Trig. "We may need to help them, too."

Trig sniffed the ground and tracked the baby turtle's path. Joe followed. They headed for the turtles' nest.

READ & RESPOND

Main Ideas and Details

How did Trig find the turtle's nest?

_____

_____

_____

Uncle Rob looked for Joe and Trig. "Where are you?" he called.

"We're over here," said Joe. "We're watching turtles."

Uncle Rob found them by the nest. The turtles were working hard. They had to dig their way out of the slippery sand.

READ & RESPOND

Main Ideas and Details

Why were the turtles working hard?

_____

_____

_____

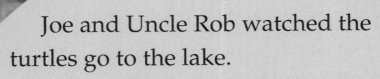

Joe and Uncle Rob watched the turtles go to the lake.

"They will be safe now," said Joe.

"It's good that you found that first turtle," said Uncle Rob. "Otherwise, they all might have been in trouble."

"Trig found it!" said Joe.

READ & RESPOND   Make Inferences

Why does Uncle Rob say that the turtles might have been in trouble?

_____

_____

_____

Reread and Respond

1 What is this story mostly about?

_____

_____

_____

Hint

For a clue, read
every page.

2 Why were the turtle eggs in the sand?

_____

_____

_____

Hint

For a clue, see
page 218.

3 What might have happened if Trig had not found
the turtle?

_____

_____

_____

Hint

For a clue, see
page 219.

Fire Safety Day

by John Berry

Randy walked to school. He was glad.
His class had gym today. He loved gym.
They would play games. They would
kick balls. Best of all, they would tumble.
Randy was ready to practice somersaults
and cartwheels.

READ & RESPOND   Make and Confirm Predictions

What do you think Randy will do in gym today?

_____

_____

_____

When he got to the gym, the gray mats were not out. They were stacked against the wall.

Mrs. Nelson was standing with two people from the fire station.

"Good morning," she said. "Today we have a special treat."

READ & RESPOND

Make and Confirm Predictions

What do you think the "special treat" is? Use the text to help you make a guess.

_____

_____

"These firefighters will talk to us about fire safety," said Mrs. Nelson. "They will teach us some rules. We will learn how to avoid fires. We will also learn what to do if there is a fire."

Randy was sad. He liked gym a lot. Now he would have to wait until next week.

READ & RESPOND

Make and Confirm Predictions

Do you think Randy will stay sad for the whole story? Explain.

_____

_____

_____

Ingrid came over. She was Randy's buddy. "What's wrong?" Ingrid said.

"Why do we have to learn about fire safety?" Randy said. "That's no fun."

"It may not be fun," she said. "Still, it's good to know."

"Maybe," he said. "I wanted to do tumbling today."

READ & RESPOND

Make and Confirm Predictions

Do you think Randy will change his mind about fire safety? Explain.

_____

_____

_____

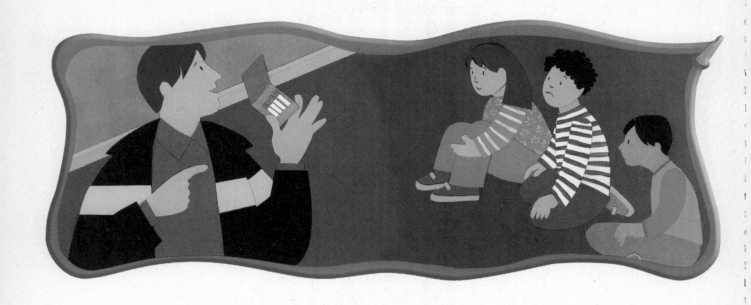

"Good morning," Chief Sims said. "We want you to be safe. The best rule is to avoid fires. Don't play with matches. They start fires."

Officer Jones gave a speech about smoke alarms. "Every house needs a smoke alarm," she said. "They save lives."

Main Ideas and Details

What does Chief Sims say is the best rule for staying safe in a fire?

_____

_____

_____

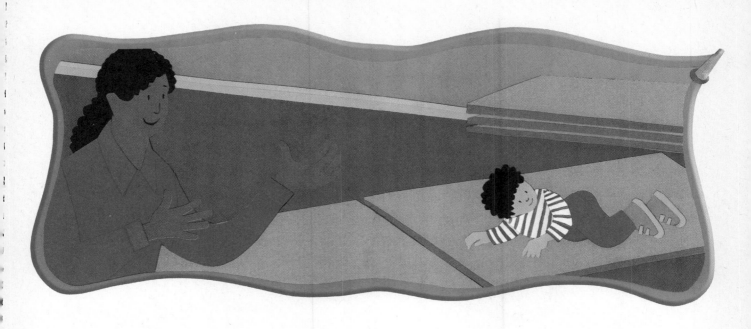

"Now let's learn what to do if your clothes catch on fire," said Officer Jones. She pulled out the gray mats. "First, stop moving. Then drop to the floor. Then roll back and forth. Who wants to try?"

Randy tried "stop, drop, and roll." It was just like tumbling!

Make and Confirm Predictions

Is Randy still sad? Explain.

_____

_____

_____

At recess, Ingrid played with
Randy. "We learned a lot about fire
safety today," she said.

"I learned something else,"
said Randy.

"What's that?" Ingrid asked.

"It was more fun than I thought!"
he said.

READ & RESPOND

Make and Confirm Predictions

**Think about how you said Randy would feel at the end of the story.
Were you correct? Explain.**

_____

_____

Reread and Respond

1 Why is Randy disappointed after he gets to school?

_____

_____

_____

Hint

See pages 228 and 229.

2 Why should every house have a smoke alarm?

_____

_____

_____

Hint

See page 230.

3 What changes Randy's mind about fire safety?

_____

_____

_____

Hint

See pages 231 and 232.

The Twelve Months

adapted by Judy Rosenbaum   *Based on a Czech fairy tale*

Marta lived with her stepsister, Vanda, and her stepmother. Marta was not treated well at all. She did all the housework. Vanda never had to do anything.

One December day, Vanda said, "I want strawberries. Go out and get me some!"

Marta didn't know what to do. Nothing grew in winter! Still, she went to look in the woods. She carried some bread for her lunch.

READ & RESPOND   **Story Structure**

Who is the main character in the story?

_____

_____

_____

Snow was on the ground. The trees were bare. Marta walked and walked. Then she came to a campfire. Twelve people sat around it.

Marta greeted the people politely. They bowed to her. They made a place for her by their warm fire. This is how people treated travelers long ago.

READ & RESPOND

Make Connections

How many people were around the campfire?
What else do you know that has this number?

_____

_____

Marta shared her bread with the strangers. The oldest man asked why she was in the woods. She explained her task.

The oldest man said, "June, help her." A woman pointed at the ground. Right away, a strawberry plant sprouted up through the snow. Soon, it had ripe, red berries.

Now Marta knew these people were not ordinary. They were the Twelve Months! The oldest man was December. The woman who made the strawberries grow was the month of June.

READ & RESPOND   Story Structure

What does Marta learn about the people by the campfire?

_____

_____

_____

Marta was overjoyed. She picked the berries. "Thank you!" she said.

Vanda met Marta at the door of their home. She grabbed the berries and ate them all. Then the questions started. "Where did you get these? Who gave them to you? Why didn't you bring more?"

Marta did not tell Vanda about the Months. She just said, "The berries were growing in the woods."

READ & RESPOND

Make Connections

Think about a time you discovered something special. How does that help you understand why Marta didn't tell Vanda about the months?

_____

_____

The next day, Marta's stepmother said, "I want roses."

Marta got ready to go. After she had left, Vanda said, "Mama, I don't trust Marta. I'm sure she has concealed something out in the woods. I think she has hidden something valuable, and I want it! I'll look for the flowers myself."

Vanda put on her warm coat. She carried a basket of food for herself.

READ & RESPOND

Story Structure

Why does Vanda follow Marta into the woods?

_____

_____

_____

It was easy to follow Marta's tracks in the snow. Soon Vanda saw the twelve people around the campfire. She didn't see any strawberries growing. So she didn't think she had reached the right place.

"Hello, traveler. What are you doing out on this cold day?" asked one of the men. Vanda didn't know it, but he was September.

"None of your business," Vanda said rudely. Then she walked away. She didn't share any of her food.

READ & RESPOND

Story Structure

What does Vanda see after she follows the tracks?

_____

_____

_____

December raised his hand. Heavy snow began to fall. It took Vanda hours to get home. Of course, she never found any roses.

A week later, Marta left the house for good. She went away to find a better life. She left two things behind. One was a note saying goodbye. The other was a bunch of roses.

READ & RESPOND   **Make Connections**

Does this story remind you of any other stories you know? What kind of story is this?

_____

_____

Reread and Respond

1 **What is the first thing that Marta must find in the woods?**

Hint
For clues, see page 234.

_____

_____

_____

2 **What different things do June and December cause to happen?**

Hint
For clues, see pages 236 and 240.

_____

_____

_____

3 **What does December think of Vanda? How do you know?**

Hint
For clues, see pages 239 and 240.

_____

_____

_____

Credits

10-16 (t) *torn paper border* ©Houghton Mifflin Harcourt; 10 *photo album* ©Stockdisk/Getty Images; 11 *indigenous family* ©Mona Makela/Shutterstock; 10 *balloons* ©Houghton Mifflin Harcourt; 11 *girl gazing* ©Getty Images; 11 *indigenous family* ©Edward S. Curtis Collection/Library of Congress Prints & Photographs Division; 11 *Dakota woman* ©Edward S. Curtis Collection/Library of Congress Prints & Photographs Division; 10 *black photo album* ©C Squared Studios/Photodisc/Getty Images; 11 *balloons* ©Houghton Mifflin Harcourt; 12 *balloons* ©Houghton Mifflin Harcourt; 12 *Santa Fe train* ©Houghton Mifflin Harcourt; 12 *crown* ©Comstock Images/Getty Images; 13 *teddy bear* ©Photodisc/Getty Images; 13 *toy robots* ©Houghton Mifflin Harcourt; 13 *tricycle* ©C Squared Studios/Photodisc/Getty Images; 14 *corn* ©iStockPhoto.com; 14 *chili peppers* ©Pipa100/Dreamstime; 14 *mango* ©Stockbyte/Getty Images; 14 *beans* ©Photodisc/Getty Images; 14 *shopping cart* ©Photodisc/Getty Images; 15 *tomato* ©anna1311/istock/Getty Images Plus/Getty Images; 15 *eggplant* ©Paul Williams -Funkystock/imageBROKER/Corbis; 15 *leaves* ©Artville/Getty Images; 15 *watermelon* ©C Squared Studios/Photodisc/Getty Images; 15 *potatoes* ©Artville/Getty Images; 15 *green beans* ©Photodisc/Getty Images; 16 *guitar* ©Nikolai Sorokin/Fotolia; 16 *balloons* ©Houghton Mifflin Harcourt; 17 *drum* ©Photodisc/Getty Images; 17 *blue drum* ©Houghton Mifflin Harcourt; 18 *rocket ship* ©Photodisc/Getty Images; 18 *baseball glove* ©C Squared Studios/Photodisc/Getty Images; 20 *flying spaceship* ©Photodisc/Getty Images; 21 *toy rocket* ©Photodisc/Getty Images; 22 *toy flying saucer* ©Getty Images; 22 *swirl sky* ©Albert J. Copley/Getty Images; 23 *toy rocket* ©Stock Up/Shutterstock; 23 *starry sky* ©Photodisc/Getty Images; 24 *stars* ©Photodisc/Stocktrek Images, Inc./Getty Images; 27 *gifts* ©C Squared Studios/Photodisc/Getty Images; 27 *stationary* ©Jack Holtel/Photographik/Houghton Mifflin Harcourt; 27 *child's drawing* ©Basileus/Shutterstock; 28 *tree* ©kpboonjit/Shutterstock; 28 *red ribbon* ©Houghton Mifflin Harcourt; 28 *birthday party invitation* ©Houghton Mifflin Harcourt; 29 *child's drawing of house* ©Houghton Mifflin Harcourt; 29 *party hats* ©Corbis; 29 *gifts* ©C Squared Studios/Photodisc/Getty Images; 30 *rope swing* ©Stockbyte/Getty Images; 31 *nest*

©Houghton Mifflin Harcourt; 31 *red ribbon* ©Houghton Mifflin Harcourt; 32 *mailbox* (cr) ©Photodisc/Getty Images; 33 *bird building nest* ©William Leaman/Alamy; 34 *snow boots* ©Stockdisk/Getty Images; 35 *snow shoes* ©Photodisc/Getty Images; 39 *Sled* ©Artville/Getty Images; 40 *skis and poles* ©Artville/Getty Images; 66 *Texas landscape* ©Digital Vision/Getty Images; 69 *baseball stadium* ©Mike Liu/Shutterstock; 70 *tickets* ©Photodisc/Getty Images; 72 *NYC skyline* ©Corbis; 81 *foliage* ©Getty Images; 91 *gardening tools* ©Houghton Mifflin Harcourt; 92 *garden tools* ©Artville/Getty Images; 92 *watering can* ©Houghton Mifflin Harcourt; 93 *yellow paint* ©Corbis; 94 *paint cans* ©Houghton Mifflin Harcourt; 98 *dog family* ©GK Hart/Vikki Hart/Stockbyte/Getty Images; 99 *washing the dog* ©Photodisc/Getty Images; 99 *brush and bone* ©Houghton Mifflin Harcourt; 100 *girl holding kitten* ©Corbis; 101 *cat and groceries* ©Getty Images; 102 *girl feeding fish* ©Comstock/Getty Images; 102-103 *goldfish* ©Yasuhide Fumoto/Getty Images; 104 *cat looking down in bowl* ©Jupiterimages/i2i/Alamy Images; 105 *sleeping puppies* ©DAJ/Getty Images; 114-120 (bkgd) *wheatfield* ©Robert Glusic/Getty Images; 114 *farmhouse* ©J.R. Bale/Alamy; 115 *scything the hay* ©Chronicle/Alamy; 119 *McCormick Reaper Manufactory* ©Wisconsin Historical Society; 119 *Cyrus McCormick* ©Science History Society/Alamy; 122 *scallop shell* ©Digital Vision/Getty Images; 122 *starfish* ©Stockdisk/Getty Images; 123 *two starfish* ©Photodisc/Getty Images; 123 *seashell* ©Jules Frazier/Photodisc/Getty Images; 126 *Hermit Crab* ©Krissy VanAlstyne/Shutterstock; 130 *turkey sandwich* ©Spencer Jones/Getty Images; 131 *mung bean sprouts* ©Artville/Getty Images; 131 *alfalfa sprouts* ©Artville/Getty Images; 131 *radish sprouts* ©Artville/Getty Images; 132-133 (bkgd) *sprout* ©DAJ/Getty Images; 133 *sprouts* ©Getty Images; 134 *alfalfa sprouts* ©Corbis; 135 *tap with running water* ©Photodisc/Getty Images; 136 *pole bean sprouts* ©Siede Preis/Photodisc/Getty Images; 137 *sprouts* ©Getty Images; 146-152 (bkgd) earth ©Stocktrek/Photodisc/Getty Images;146 *Rubik's cube* ©Photodisc/Getty Images; 146 *backgammon* ©Photodisc/Getty Images; 147 *checkers* ©Comstock/Getty Images; 147 *game mancala* ©Houghton Mifflin Harcourt; 148 *board game pachisi* ©Mangala Shenvi/Dreamstime; 149 *top*

©Photodisc/Getty Images; 149 *string* ©Houghton Mifflin Harcourt; 150 *soccer ball* ©Photodisc/Getty Images; 151 *game Go* ©Houghton Mifflin Harcourt; 151 *chess* ©Photodisc/Getty Images; 152 *colorful marbles* ©Houghton Mifflin Harcourt; 153 *soccer ball* ©Photodisc/Getty Images; 154 *retail store* ©Corbis; 155 *yarn and needles* ©Comstock/Getty Images; 156 *red yarn* ©Brand X Pictures/Getty Images; 157 *knitting in progress* ©Houghton Mifflin Harcourt; 158 *clock* ©Comstock/Getty Images; 159 *American wirehair* ©Artville/Getty Images; 159 *balls of yarn* ©Picsfive/Shutterstock; 160 *happy family* ©Blue Jean Images/Getty Images; 161 *red yarn* ©Brand X Pictures/Getty Images; 170-176 *storm blowing trees* (bkgd) ©Blend Images - REB Images/Brand X Pictures/Getty Images; 171 *red candle* ©Houghton Mifflin Harcourt; 171 *water bottle* ©Houghton Mifflin Harcourt; 172 *radio* ©Houghton Mifflin Harcourt; 172 *television* ©Photodisc/Getty Images; 173 *masking tape* ©Houghton Mifflin Harcourt; 174 *board games* ©Houghton Mifflin Harcourt; 175 *tree branches* ©Photodisc/Getty Images; 176 *snowplow clearing road* ©Corbis; 176 *tornado* ©Corbis; 176 *hurricane* ©Photodisc/Getty Images; 186-193 (repeating) *leaf* ©Nguyen Thai/Shutterstock; 194 *magnifying glass* ©Artville/Getty Images; 195 *books* ©Artville/Getty Images; 196 *inkwell and pen* ©C Squared Studios/Getty Images; 196 *pad* ©Getty Images; 198 *pad/folder* ©Photodisc/Getty Images; 199 *books* ©Photodisc/Getty Images; 200 *braille* ©Photodisc/Getty Images; 202 *girl playing bongo* ©Jose Luis Pelaez, Inc./Blend Images/Corbis; 203 *African Claves* ©Photodisc/Getty Images; 203 *maracas* ©Getty Images; 204 *girl playing recorder* ©Photodisc/Getty Images; 205 *Tuba* ©Artville/Getty Images; 206 *violin and bow* ©C Squared Studios/Photodisc/Getty Images; 207 *hands clapping* ©Photodisc/Getty Images; 208 *music class* ©Ryan McVay/Photodisc/Getty Images; 209 *tambourine* ©Comstock/Getty Images; 218-224 (bkgd) *water* ©Corbis; 226-232 (bkgd) *fire* ©Photodisc/Getty Images; 227 *fire extinguisher* ©Photodisc/Getty Images; 228 *firefighter's helmet* ©Photodisc/Getty Images; 229 *rubber boots* ©Photodisc/Getty Images; 230 *smoke alarm* ©Photodisc/Getty Images; 232 *firetruck* ©Houghton Mifflin Harcourt.